"A timely book that will be a real help for couples needing advice on how to make their special situation work. I loved Marita's warm and funny anecdotes regarding her own marriage and Chuck's sound advice given in a professional manner. Their different personalities make for great reading."

Carole Lewis
National Director, First Place

"The authors show that while opposites sometimes attack, they also attract. The principles and practical helps will help modern marriages not only survive—but thrive—as couples discover a supernatural joy in going the second mile."

Rebecca Barlow Jordan,
Speaker, Author of *At Home in My Heart*

"A must-read for today's Christian couples. This is an honest, open, down-to-earth guide for couples who dare to have marriages that are authentic and adventurous—marriages built around intimacy with Christ. It addresses in a fresh, practical way the problems that every couple has long struggled with."

Bill Welte
President and Executive Director of America's KESWICK

"Every modern marriage can benefit from this well-written book that has something for everyone. The real-life examples provide practical, spiritual, and emotional help and support for nearly every situation. I highly recommend it."

Karen O'Connor
Author

"Does your marriage need a boost? Is it outside traditional roles and schedules? Then read *Love Extravagantly* for thought-provoking encouragement, practical insight, and downright fun."

Sandra P. Aldrich
Author of *Men Read Newspapers, Not Minds*

"Pragmatic Marita does it again. She first experiments and then she exports principles that enhance a marriage—not as marriage *should be*, but as it is in *real life*. No Ozzie-and-Harriet here, just workable answers for nourishing a relationship."

Lee Ezell
Author and Speaker

"From the time Marita came into this world, I have loved her extravagantly as only a mother can. I have encouraged her creativity and enthused over her sense of humor. This book is her best yet! She and Chuck give practical and inspirational examples of today's modern marriages. This book will widen your perception of current trends and give you some new ways to refresh your own marriage and explain it to your mother."

Florence Littauer
President of CLASS Speakers, Inc., Author and Speaker

"Marita and Chuck live out their love and show you how to also—even when marriage isn't 'business as usual.' Actually, every marriage is different and a challenge. In a creative way, along with an abundance of illuminating ideas, practical biblical principles, and encouraging examples, this husband-wife team will give you the inspiration and jump start you need to keep on in your marriage—no matter how unusual you think your relationship is."

Kathy Collard Miller
Author of *Why Do I Put So Much Pressure on Myself?*

"*Love Extravagantly* is the antithesis of our culture and the essence of God's prototype and example for marriage. As he loves the church extravagantly, extending grace and giving, we are to love each other amid the cacophony and complexity of modern life! In a fast paced, personalized, practical format, Marita and Chuck give us God's perspective for the 21st century. A must read for marriage excellence!"

Naomi Rhode, CSP CPAE
Professional Speaker, Vice Chair, Smart Health,

"What Marita has to say in the preface alone is worth the price of this book! Practicing extravagant love will revolutionize any marriage."

Candy Davison
Women's Ministries Coordinator, Sandy Cove Ministries

"An excellent book that finally talks about today's *real* marriages: anecdotal, insightful, specific advice. A winning combination for study as an individual couple or group."

Dianna Booher
Speaker and Author of *Worth of a Woman's Words* and
Communication With Confidence

"Marita Littauer and Chuck Noon boldly forged through uncharted waters in terms of applying biblical principles to many different marriage and family scenarios. They have successfully applied these principles to discover what 'happily ever after' means in post-modern America. Love Extravagantly will be a great help to those seeking answers for marriages."

Skip and Lenya Heitzig
Senior Pastor, Calvary Chapel of Albuquerque

"The vignettes in *Love Extravagantly* are like looking into a mirror and discovering that someone else has experienced situations like yours. The wisdom and advice give one hope and practical ways to find positive solutions. The practical application steps become the means to incorporate change into life. Chuck and Marita have pulled together an amazing book."

Betty Southard
Speaker and Author of *Come As You Are* and
The Grandmother Book

MARITA LITTAUER is a professional speaker with over twenty years of experience. She is the author of ten books, including *Personality Puzzle*, *Come As You Are* (with Betty Southard), and *You've Got What It Takes*. She is the president of CLASServices Inc., an organization that provides resources, training, and promotion for speakers and authors.

CHUCK NOON is a licensed professional counselor who has worked with hundreds of families in a variety of settings. Chuck and Marita have been married since 1983 and make their home in Albuquerque, New Mexico.

For additional information on Marita or CLASServices, please call 800-433-6633 or visit *www.classervices.com*.

MARITA LITTAUER
CHUCK NOON

BETHANYHOUSE
Minneapolis, Minnesota

Love Extravagantly
Copyright © 2001
Marita Littauer

Cover design by Koechel Peterson & Associates.
Cover photo: Photonica, photographer Shinya Yoshimori

Published by Bethany House Publishers
A Ministry of Bethany Fellowship International
11400 Hampshire Avenue South, Bloomington, Minnesota 55438
www.bethanyhouse.com

Printed in the United States of America by
Bethany Press International, Bloomington, Minnesota 55438

Library of Congress Cataloging-in-Publication Data

Littauer, Marita.
    Love extravagantly : making the modern marriage work / by Marita Littauer.
      p. cm.
    ISBN 0-7642-2276-7 (pbk.)
    1. Marriage—United States. 2. Marriage—United States—Religious aspects—Christianity.
3. Remarriage—United States. I. Title.
    HQ734 .L59   2001
    306.85'0973—dc21   2001002253

Contents

Foreword

Marita Littauer is one of those rare women in the twenty-first century who truly loves her husband with extravagance. I used to tell her, "Marita, you spoil your husband." But that was before I witnessed the powerful differences that loving extravagantly can make in a marriage. Now I have a totally different attitude when she "pampers" her husband, Chuck. I'm more likely to comment, "I hope if I ever remarry we will love each other like that."

Although I've known Marita for eleven years, it is in recent years that we have become best friends. Marita was the one I called when doctors found my ovarian tumor. She was the one I telephoned when an editor told me I would be receiving my first book contract. Marita has shared my joys and my sorrows, and in turn I have been with her during some good times and some difficult ones. Having stayed in Marita's home and talked with her weekly, I can promise you her marriage, like most, has had its challenges. But regardless of the situation she's facing, her commitment to her marriage and to love with extravagance is evident.

As a divorced person, I wish someone would have taught me this concept years before my separation. Maybe it would have made a difference in my life and in my son's life. Although I can't change the past, I can, like you, learn new skills to impact the future. And who better to teach us than someone who practices them daily? Therefore, it is without reservation that I recommend this book, knowing it will be a blessing to you and your marriage.

—Georgia Shaffer
Speaker and Author of
A Gift of Mourning Glories

Preface

While writing "Celebrate Your Path," a chapter in *You've Got What It Takes* about the value of a mission statement, I looked at my own life. I had a defining statement—theme—for my professional ventures, but I did not have a personal one. I knew how valuable my professional statement was, so I could see the importance of a personal one—even recommending this to my readers—but I did not have one myself. I mulled this over for several days, focusing on the need for a personal purpose statement, the "path" of my personal life.

At the time I was attending a women's Bible study on the book of Ephesians. As part of my preparation for the study, I would read the assigned chapter in several different versions of the Bible. One night I read Ephesians 5 in *The Message*. I wasn't looking for a personal mission statement, although it was still in the back of my mind. I was simply preparing for the lesson the next day.

But as I read, this verse jumped out at me and I instantly knew it was my personal path—at least for now; "Observe how Christ loved us. His love is not cautious but extravagant. He didn't love in order to get something from us but to give everything of himself to us. Love like that" (v. 1). As I read that, I knew that my personal mission is to love my husband with extravagance, not to get, but to give everything of myself. As I cook breakfast or dinner, as I do the dishes, as I do the laundry, I can give something of myself, not expecting to get in return. My husband has had a rough time in the last year. He has not been in a place to be able to give much. But I am. I wrote that verse on my bathroom mirror to remind me of my mission.

I find that I have to frequently repeat this verse to myself, as it is contrary to my human nature. As Glenn T. Stanton says in his book *Why Marriage Matters*, "The depth and quality of love can only be sustained by a conscious act of will; it never simply happens."[1]

Shortly after embracing this idea of loving extravagantly, I had to put it to the test. Chuck has a large radio-controlled model airplane that has been a part of his life for over thirty years—he started building it when he was sixteen and finally finished it twenty-five years later. We have painstakingly moved it from house to house. He has too much of himself invested in it to risk flying it. With a five-foot wingspan, you cannot just tuck it any place. In our current home it hangs near the peak of the cathedral ceiling in the family room. Bright red with Red Baron-like decals, it is sure to be noticed. Since it is important to Chuck, I have accepted it as a conversation piece—and you can be sure it is! It has traveled with us to eight different houses.

Recently he took the airplane to a model airplane show. He spent hours cleaning off the accumulated dust that had firmly attached itself to every surface. The plane was very popular at the show, and he discovered how valuable it really is. Before he put it back on its hook, he wanted to protect it. So he covered the body and wings with plastic dry cleaning bags, advertising and all.

I like my home to look like a showplace; even having the airplane there is an act of compromise and love. Having it covered with baggy dry cleaning bags with words on them went too far. "I'll never be able to entertain again!" I wailed to him. After my outburst, which I knew was an overreaction, I went outside and trimmed my roses. As I took a deep breath, "love extravagantly" came to mind. Does it really matter if the airplane has bags over it? What is more important, that my husband be happy or that I have a lovely home? Hmm . . . that was tough. *Love extravagantly*, I told myself. I came back in and apologized—ready to accept the dry cleaning bags. Meanwhile, he had decided that I was right and it really was ugly. He had taken the plane down, removed the dry cleaning bags, and was replacing them with clear plastic wrap that clings tightly to every horizontal curve and doesn't even show!

Ah, the power of a personal mission statement: not cautious but extravagant, not to get but to give. What changes do you need to make to love your spouse extravagantly? Make it your personal purpose statement. Love extravagantly.

I told this story in *You've Got What It Takes,* and I include the story every time I speak on that book. Repeatedly after I share the story, people tell me that "love extravagantly" is what they needed to hear.

The first time I shared it I was speaking at a women's conference in Oregon. At the end of the day, a woman came up to me and said, "Out of everything that has gone on here today, 'love extravagantly' is what I am taking home with me." I thanked her and smiled. I realized I had hit upon something that wasn't just important to me; it resonated with my audiences. I shared the same message with a group of women in Phoenix. At the end, an older woman came up to me and said, "What you shared about loving extravagantly was for me." She explained that her husband was terminally ill and she was his caretaker. She needed to remember to love extravagantly.

After hearing the "love extravagantly" story at a women's conference, a woman sent me the following e-mail: *"Brad has given me an opportunity to love extravagantly!!! While I was at the conference, he must have gotten bored, because he decided to take all of his old LPs out of their box in the garage, along with his old turntable. The turntable has replaced our cassette deck on top of the stereo in our living room (for all to see), and his albums are stacked in the hall. I'm not talking five or ten or even twenty-five albums—I'm guessing there are at least two hundred or more (I don't have the heart to count). They are not something you can pretend to overlook. So . . . before I called him at work to ask how long they would be sitting there, I decided to love extravagantly, as you have challenged me to do, and not say a word."*

As I continue to speak on the message of *You've Got What It Takes*, I've found the need for the love extravagantly principle to be universal. What began as a small part of my previous book has grown into a book of its own. On the following pages you will see snapshots of many marriages and how following Christ's example—not to get but to give, not cautious but extravagant—can make a significant difference. From their examples, you can apply the same ideas to your own marriage and expect similar results. With all the changes in today's family structure, couples need something more than just love to make their marriages work. They need to love extravagantly!

The Average American Family

"The demographic changes of the past century make it difficult to speak of an average American family."[1]

*E*ach morning I drag my body out of bed, and after a brief stop in the bathroom, I head for the kitchen. Harley, my husband's raucous schnauzer, jumps off the bed and follows me. He passes the kitchen and trots to the sliding glass door, where he waits for me to let him out. I unlock the door and he bounds out as if there will be some new and exciting thing that was not there the day before. Lacking his enthusiasm for morning, I trudge back into the kitchen, fill the teakettle, and place it on the stove.

I dump yesterday's coffee grounds out of the French press, rinse it, and add three scoops of fresh coffee—on weekends I grind fresh beans. I select one of my husband's favorite mugs bearing the likeness of a schnauzer. I choose a tall porcelain cup for myself, open the package of my favorite tea, and place the bag in the cup.

While waiting for the water to boil, I clean up any dishes from the night before or empty the dishwasher. If neither dish duty needs to be done, I join Harley in the backyard and check out my roses or see how far my morning glories have climbed since the day before. While surveying the backyard, I hear the teakettle whistle in the distance and return to the kitchen. There I pour the hot water over the grounds in the French press and into the cup containing my tea bag. Usually by this point, my schnauzer, Tucker, has surfaced and needs to go outside—but only if I go with him. If I don't go out too, he'll wait until later.

When the coffee is ready, I fill Chuck's cup, add some cream, and pour the rest of the coffee into a thermal carafe. With his coffee in one hand and my tea in the other, I head back to the bathroom. By now Chuck is in the shower. I hand his coffee in to him. Through the sound of the spray I hear, "Thanks, Rabbit."

While he showers, I wash my face, put in my contacts, and put on my makeup. As he dresses, I go back to the kitchen and cook his breakfast—a fresh, hot, real Belgian waffle (see recipe, appendix B) with bacon or sausage. We eat together while flipping through the selection of morning shows in search of news and carrying on as much conversation as the early hour allows. After rubbing my shoulders in thanks, Chuck leaves for work. I do the dishes. Then I get dressed, feed the dogs, lock up the house, and go to work.

If we were an average American family—if there was such a thing—that is what would happen each morning at your house too! However, if you are like most of my girlfriends, you are exhausted just reading about the first hour of my day. If you are like most of my girlfriends' husbands, you want to move in.

Equilibrium

Our morning ritual is what works for us. It is part of the balance that has made our marriage successful over the last eighteen years. Chuck says he'll hurt himself shaving if he doesn't have coffee first thing in the morning. I am not caffeine dependent so I bring it to him. His stomach and mind need good fuel to function effectively. I like to cook, so I make him what he likes—even though many days I make eggs for myself. Chuck jokes that he likes his breakfast so much he has chosen John 21:12a as his life verse: "Jesus said to them, 'Come and eat breakfast'" (NKJV).

My sister and her husband have just celebrated their twenty-sixth anniversary. A year ago I visited them for five days. As I observed their life together, I was struck by how different it was from my marriage. Randy makes coffee for both of them while Lauren is still in bed. If breakfast is made, usually Randy does it. Our morning routines are merely a sampling of the differences in our marriages. Their marriage is different, but it too is successful. Over the years they have developed a pattern that works for them with their personalities and their place in life.

After observing my sister's marriage, I thought about my parents. They have been married forty-nine years. When I stay in their home or travel with them, I see their relationship in action. Their marriage has taken on its own characteristics; they have created their own formula that works for them. My father takes care of every little need for my mother to the point that if she calls me, he dials the phone, says hello, and then hands the phone off to her. I'd feel suffocated under such circumstances. She feels pampered and special.

When my friend Eva Marie read about my morning routine, she said,

> If I got up and made a waffle for Dennis, he would think I had charged too much on my Macy's credit card and was trying to soften the blow. Or perhaps that I wrecked the car! In fact, in my house, I rarely cook! We eat what we can, when we can! For us, it works . . . especially now that there are only the two of us.

Each of our marriages is different, yet each has stood the test of time—each is successful. Over the years, in each of our marriages, we have developed our own balance. We have created what I like to call an equilibrium that works for each individual couple. While this parity brings about a marriage with which each couple is happy, we could not trade places and expect the same procedures or rituals to work for the other couples, as each union is made up of different factors. What works for Chuck and me will not automatically have the same results in *your* marriage. Your marriage needs its own equilibrium.

A few months ago my sister and her husband visited us. After watching my marriage, I'd guess that my sister wouldn't want to change places with me. Both Lauren and Chuck would be waiting for someone to bring them their coffee! While Chuck and I have created an equilibrium that works for us, I know most of my friends wouldn't want my marriage either!

So if I have a marriage no one would want to replicate, why am I writing a book on marriage? I am writing this not because I am an expert, not because I have the model of a perfect marriage, not because I have all the answers. I am writing because I realize that there is no perfect marriage, no average American family. I am writing because I understand that each union brings to the table different needs, expectations, backgrounds, and personalities[2] that make every marriage unique. As such, no one book or one formula will work for everyone. Each couple needs to find their own equilibrium.

The Modern Marriage

My marriage has some specific characteristics that make it different from many of my friends' marriages. Yet it also has traits that I find are like so many other marriages today. My marriage, and possibly yours, little resembles what was modeled in my youth as the ideal marriage. When I was growing up, television wanted us to believe that all marriages fit a certain mold: first marriage for both spouses. Husband goes off to work every day and is the sole breadwinner. His job is secure and he works for the same company all his life. He is the leader, the disciplinarian (remember "Wait till your father gets home"?), and the decision-maker in the family. Wife stays home and takes care of the children and her husband. She is sweet, gracious, and agreeable to whatever her husband suggests. I call this family the Ozzie-and-Harriet model, named for the perfect television family of the '50s and '60s. An article in *USA Today* affirmed the demise of the this model,

> "The days of the traditional Ozzie-and-Harriet family are pretty much done," says Melanie Fox, principal of an elementary school in Coral Gables, Florida. "We have 750 children in this school, and the majority come from homes with at least one divorce."[3]

My friend Kim says,

> I remember watching my parents' Ozzie-and-Harriet marriage, and while I respected them, I did not want to follow in my mother's footsteps! As it turns out, our lives are very different. But we are both happy. However, I can't figure out how she fills her days now!

Those of us who do not fit the Ozzie-and-Harriet model have what I call a modern marriage. This model may include a marriage where both spouses work and produce an income. They may work outside the home or have a home-based business, but they both produce income—perhaps the woman makes more than her husband does or he works for her. It might include a marriage that is a second or third marriage for one or both spouses. There may be ex-spouse issues or step-children that factor in to the marriage. It might include a marriage where the couple has chosen to be childless. Due to career changes or a need to care for an aging parent, spouses may have to live a commuter marriage for a period of time. The modern marriage could be something as subtle as the wife having the stronger personality. Because each marriage is unique, these are just a sampling of the situations that may constitute the modern marriage.

When I shared the concept of this book with someone at a conference, she was surprised that there was a need for such a book. She asked,

> Who will read it? In Texas all of my gal friends do not work and their hubbies are the primary breadwinners. Once in my marriage my husband was laid off, and I sat around and prayed and prayed and he networked and networked, talking to

people who needed tax work. I am not educated like I wish I were (only a junior college degree). His family is wealthy so they paid our house payment and I worked wherever I could at odd jobs—mostly taking care of elderly people. So I cannot relate to gals being the breadwinner and making more money. I wonder if that is a West Coastish phenomenon? In the South gals are not as educated and just have babies and clean house and look pretty and maybe inherit money. Most of my gal friends do not work.

Proof that Ozzie and Harriet do still exist.

No, it is not just a West Coast phenomenon. Perhaps the South does have a higher share of the traditional family and the West more renegades. But I have found couples struggling with issues unique to the modern marriage all over the country—even Texas!

As an author, books are my world. When I review books on marriage, I find most of them assume that marriages are still the Ozzie-and-Harriet model. I find this model rare today. Recent research shows that the percentage of American households made up of married couples with children in the home dropped from 45 percent in the early 1970s to just 26 percent in 1998.[4] For many of us, the principles and ideals outlined in the excellent books available on marriage do not apply. One I just read had a list of things a woman could do to show her husband that she loves him and vice versa. Item number ninety-five on her list says to send him cards at his place of work, and number ninety-six suggests that she stuff his suitcase with love notes when he travels. Yet his list doesn't suggest the same. What if she is the one who travels, as in my case?

If, like me, you have read some of these books and felt frustrated because they seem so out of touch with the reality of your household, *Love Extravagantly* is for you. Since there are many wonderful books out there that address the basics of a traditional marriage, I have chosen to address those of us who feel left out. This book will look at a cross section of unique marriage situations—those issues that many of our parents didn't have to face—and help you find the equilibrium that is right for your particular set of circumstances. And if your modern marriage issues don't match up exactly with those presented, you'll still find principles that apply; see chapter 18, "From the Head to the Heart," for guidelines to help you custom tailor the issues, insights, and interactions to fit.

I have what I call a modern marriage, but because of what had been modeled for me as a child, when I entered into it I had traditional expectations. The two did not meet. I had to make adjustments in my expectations of what I thought my marriage would be. But there was no guide for me as to how to make my modern marriage work. Many of us base our marriages on an unrealistic image.

When counseling couples, my husband, Chuck, asks them to paint a word picture of their childhood model of marriage. He asks them to use an analogy of a television show, a fairy tale, or storybook that reflects their view of marriage. The response is often something like *Father Knows Best, Ozzie and Harriet, Leave It to Beaver,* or *Cinderella.* Next, he asks them, "Is that what you *expect* from your current marriage? Is that what you *want* from your marriage today?" After a pause in which the lights go on, the couple usually realizes that they have unconsciously had a fairy tale "happily-ever-after" expectation of their real-life marriage that has resulted in fighting and disagreements. Once the couple is able to acknowledge that their expectations are unrealistic—and often not even really what they want today, they can accept where they are and build from there.

When discussing this book with my friend Jan, she said,

> I wish there had been a book like this available fifteen years ago. I might still be married today. I tried so hard to be Harriet, but that was just not me. My expectations were unrealistic. I was the strong personality. I tried so hard to be sweet and submissive, to bake cookies and have dinner ready on time. I thought I was the only one who struggled with what I perceived as the right way. But that was all I knew to do.

As you read the scenarios in the following chapters, you will see that you are not alone—as Jan thought she was. You will see that other couples have issues too. But most importantly, you will see that when you care enough to apply the principle of loving extravagantly—loving as Christ did; not to get but to give—most of the problems you face can be solved.

When I first began to develop these ideas, I shared them with my mother. She could see that I definitely had a modern marriage. I owned my own business when I got married. I have always worked outside the home (though at times my office was in the home), and I have always expected to work—in fact, I looked forward to it. At many phases of our marriage, I have been the primary breadwinner. My husband was married briefly before we met. While he is my first, and only, husband, I am his second wife. After eighteen years of marriage, we have still never felt ready to have children—we are childless by choice. I use my maiden name professionally and my married name privately. I am known as Marita Littauer and my husband as Chuck Noon. Clearly we have a modern marriage; we do not fit the Ozzie-and-Harriet model.

However, my mother proudly proclaimed that she had a "traditional marriage." I chuckled. "How do you figure?" I asked. "You work outside the home. You are the primary breadwinner. And your husband works for you."

"Oh," she replied, "I guess I was thinking of when you kids were young."

Yes, my mother was a true stay-at-home mom when I was young and my dad the only breadwinner. But the shift from then to now has created a need for a change in the balance of my parents' marriage as well. They have a new equilibrium.

As I look around, I see the modern marriage everywhere. I've just described my mother and father's marriage and mine. My sister is more traditional in that she has three sons and has made parenting her priority. Neither she nor her husband had been married before. She was twenty, he was twenty-six when they got married. However, with her strong personality, she has almost always had some type of enterprise going on. Her husband is more low-key; he owns his own business, and she has often worked with him in the store. She has had a real estate license for twenty-five years, managed a thriving real estate business for a major broker in her town, and remains active in the real estate market today. She has a sharp business mind and does bookkeeping and management consulting for several small businesses. She does newsletter design and editing for a few clients, including me. And now that her youngest is in high school and the other boys are on their own, she is interested in getting back into speaking and writing, which she did before her children were born.

My brother married later in life. He was thirty-five. It is his first marriage, but his wife had been married briefly before. She was twenty-eight. They met at work, but when they got married, company policy prevented them from both working at the same firm. She found another job. They do hope to have children someday, and she wants to create a home-based business that will allow her more flexibility so she can care for her children and work. Currently they are both working twelve hours a day, part of which is their commute. Their personalities replicate my marriage: he is more quiet and private and she is outgoing and social.

That is my family. What about my friends?

Ann and Gerry have been married seventeen years. They own a business together. They each have their own skills that have made the business a success. But they both also have different ideas about how the business should be run. While these differences have helped, they have also been a major source of stress in their marriage. It is Ann's third marriage, and she has three grown children from her first marriage. It is Gerry's second marriage, and he has no children—although he has been like a father to Ann's children, as the oldest was a teenager when they got married. Like Chuck and me, and my brother and his wife, Ann has the stronger personality and Gerry is content to be in the background.

Mark and Melody have been married for fifteen years. It is a first marriage for both. They do not have children, though they have tried and are struggling with infertility issues. After they got married, Mark felt called to the ministry. He took a position as a youth pastor at a small church and worked at a major home improvement store to pay the bills. Meanwhile Melody worked as vice president of operations for a national ministry. She was the primary breadwinner and loved her job. When Mark's small church had difficulties, he had to look for another position. Without a seminary education, his opportunities were limited. His new job required a move out of state, away from family and friends. Melody got a job at the local university, where she worked for several years. She always was eager to leave that job. Recently she did. Melody is now building her own business as an interpreter for the deaf.

Joseph and Caroline have been married for three years. It is a second marriage for both. Her daughter lives with them except for occasional visits to her father two states away. Joseph's children are with him and Caroline for two weeks and their mother the next two—which creates frequent interaction with Joseph's ex-wife. Caroline was financially successful before marrying Joseph. She is in business with her father and works out of the home. Joseph has his own thriving business.

Chip and Cindy have been married eighteen years. It is a first marriage for both. They have two children, a girl and a boy. Chip is a tax attorney. Cindy is a doctor in private practice. Cindy's mother lives with them and has helped with the children for years. Her mother has some values that are very different from those Chip and Cindy hold; they often feel they are battling her in the raising of their children.

Those are some of my friends. What about my employees?

Linda and Jim have been married for sixteen years. It is a second marriage for both. Linda has a grown son who was ten when they got married. Jim never had children. While Jim has always been the primary breadwinner, he recently chose to take an early retirement. Linda has always worked and is not yet ready to retire. Fortunately for me, she loves her job at CLASS. Jim would like to travel and take advantage of his retirement, but Linda's responsibilities require that she be in the office every day. Additionally, Jim's parents, who live several states away, are elderly with failing health. He has made several extended trips to care for them while Linda stays home and works.

Craig and Cheryl have been married twenty-two years. It is a first marriage for both. They have two teenagers. Cheryl is a nurse and Craig is a music minister. Due to some situations at his previous church, Craig found himself suddenly unemployed a couple of years ago. Together Craig and Cheryl decided that Craig would accept a position at a new church as music minister and Cheryl would go back to work full time as the primary breadwinner. Since the new church was small, Craig's position would initially be as a part-time volunteer. Hence he came to work for CLASS and Cheryl remains the primary breadwinner.

These are some of the couples in my life. Do you see any consistency? They are all different, but none fit the Ozzie-and-Harriet model. Look around. I believe you will find a similar variety of circumstances. The patterns we observed in our youth are no longer valid for many of us. The roles the media portrayed back then are no longer relevant for most of us today. The expectations society placed on our marriages aren't realistic anymore. So where are we to look for help, guidance, and answers to the unique situations of the modern marriage?

How to Use This Book

This book is as unique and modern as the marriages I hope to help. Rather than outline a specific success formula for every marriage to follow, it recognizes the premise that each marriage is unique—there is no longer an average American family. While all marriages are different, many do face similar issues and difficulties. In the following pages you will find a collection of real-life scenarios—which I've called the Issues. Gathered through the miracle of modern technology—e-mail and the Internet—these scenarios have also been reviewed by couples worldwide. Those who have faced something similar in their marriages have offered insights as to how they got through the situation and found their own equilibrium. These insights are presented with the contributors' first names only. In most cases their real names are used, however, some have asked that their identity be protected.

Additionally, therapists and other experts have given advice based on their professional experience and what they have seen work in similar situations. To make their contributions easy to identify, the professionals are identified by the use of their last name and title. Appendix C, at the end of the book, is a directory of these professionals. Please review it for more information on them and their ministries or practices.

As someone with a burden for the modern marriage, a writer, and a Personality expert, I am bringing the issues, the peer insight, and the professional advice together and adding the input on the Personality complications. (As suggested earlier, I highly recommend you review or study appendix A on Personality Types. I will be referring to them throughout the book.) While his fingers seldom touched the keyboard, my husband, Chuck Noon, a licensed therapist, has added his opinion— mostly through our dinner conversation and inline skating excursions.

The combined advice from peers and professional counselors is under the heading Insights.

At the end of each chapter, you will find activities—called Interaction—to assist you in putting the teaching into practice. If you were actually visiting a counselor, these activities would be the homework you would be asked to do before returning for the next session.

While all the scenarios are different, they have been grouped under the following headings: Career, Finances, Ex-spouse, Stepfamily, and Personal. In my marriage, most of our difficulties revolve around the Career and Finance areas. So I would read those sections but skip the section on Stepfamily, which does not apply to me. Many of my friends would spend most of their time in the Ex-spouse and Stepfamily areas.

Because this book is designed in such a way that you are encouraged to hopscotch through it, reading the sections that apply to you, some of the concepts are presented more than once. Insights too may be similar in several situations as concepts are repeated in the appropriate settings.

Chuck and I recommend that every couple use the communication exercise found in appendix D. It will be helpful for virtually every other scenario offered in *Love Extravagantly*. While certain Personality types—especially the Powerful Cholerics and the Peaceful Phlegmatics—are apt to be resistant to this type of work, it should only take about fifteen to twenty minutes a day (or an hour each week). It always pays big dividends. It is referred to in various chapters as the communication exercise.

Browse the table of contents. By reading the scenarios that most closely fit your unique situation, you will gain insight, guidance, and advice specifically applicable to you, allowing you and your spouse to create an equilibrium that works for your marriage.

1

CAREER
ISSUES

Chapter TWO

Lack of Time Together

Temporary Separations, Communication, Creative Time
Together

The Issue

*J*ohn has a job that requires him to travel five days a week, three weeks a month. A Powerful Choleric with some Perfect Melancholy, he thrives with his fast-paced, full life. His weekends are short. He usually arrives home on Friday evening; if his flight is late, the hour sometimes is past midnight. Completely exhausted after traveling from one city to another, he catches a few extra hours of sleep on Saturday morning. Then, after brunch with his wife, Joan, he heads straight to his home office to file reports from the past week and prepare for the upcoming week. Joan has her second cup of coffee, reads the morning newspaper, and cleans the kitchen, hoping this Saturday will be different—he will finish early. But the routine is unchanged.

By late afternoon he completes his work and sits down with Joan to discuss plans for Saturday night. Their routine has developed into going out to dinner with friends, going to a movie, or renting a movie and staying home. On Sunday, John joins his friends in a round of golf. Then he has a late lunch with Joan before packing his bag to leave for another week of work and travel.

Joan's job as a schoolteacher keeps her busy during the day, but her evenings are lonely. She reads, watches television, has dinner at a restaurant with friends, or telephones her parents. The companionship she expected in marriage is absent.

When they married, John was traveling two to three days a week. A few months later, he was promoted to regional sales manager and his travel schedule increased. Rather than travel four weeks out of the month, he would have one week at home. But during that week, he works in the office from early morning until late evening. Many times after dinner, he will return to the office to work on projects for the upcoming weeks. Except for having dinner together and John's sleeping at home that week, there is little difference in their weekly routine.

Joan understands the demands of John's job, but as a Popular Sanguine, she misses him and the fun they had early in their marriage. Before marriage, they had discussed having a family. John now feels they should not have a baby until his schedule is less hectic. He keeps reassuring Joan that things will not always be this way. She is concerned that their marriage is suffering from a lack of time together. Each time she brings the subject up, he argues that he is a good provider and spends as much time as possible with her.

Insights

In our global workplace, many couples have to spend more and more time apart. John's job requires that he spend large chunks of time on the road. This often happens in military families as well. Other couples are temporarily separated when one spouse has been transferred and the other has not yet found new employment. In other cases one spouse may have to spend long periods of time away meeting the needs of extended family. Whatever the circumstances that create the separation, we have chosen to address two key concerns that are important for keeping a long-distance marriage healthy: communication and creative time together.

COMMUNICATION

Most marriages suffer from lack of communication, but for couples who spend large quantities of time apart, it is especially easy for their lives to drift in different directions. For John and Joan to maintain a healthy marriage, they need to remain in contact with each other and be involved in each other's independent activities, much as they would be if they had dinner together every night.

For me, this was a concern when Chuck and I were living apart due to our jobs. As in John and Joan's case, Chuck did not seem as bothered by this as I was. For five months we saw each other only on weekends. We communicated mostly by phone and occasionally via e-mail. It seemed that the nights we felt like talking did not coincide. By the time we had our phone conversation at the end of the day, if I was tired, he wanted to talk. If I had time to talk, he was tired and short with me.

One night, when Chuck was first living in Colorado, I called him as I usually did, but he did not answer. I overreacted, first wondering where he was and whom he was with, as he had always been reachable. I tried his cell phone and couldn't get him. I got angry and then worried as the hours ticked by and I still could not reach him. When he finally answered, I was in tears. Once I calmed down and we discussed the situation, Chuck agreed that he would keep his cell phone with him and keep it on. I agreed that if I called and he was out having pizza with the other therapists, that I would not expect a full report of his day, but I would know where he was and I wouldn't worry.

However, we had to *plan* to make our usual conversations a priority. We had to call each other earlier in the evening. Originally our tendency was to place the call just before turning out the light, but we were too tired by then to share much of what went on in each other's day. As we developed a better pattern, even though I'd never met any of the boys he worked with in the residential treatment center, I felt like I knew them almost as well as he did.

Now we are back living in the same house, but I travel and am occasionally on the road for a week at a time. The day-to-day communications still take an effort to maintain. We talk on the phone almost every night when I'm gone. I leave notes for Chuck in places I know he will discover throughout my trip: in the refrigerator, under his pillow, in a book he is reading, in his organizer, under a few pairs of socks. Sometimes he sends me e-mail. It brightens my day to open up my e-mail while I am on the road and see that I have a note from Chuck.

While these ideas may sound trivial, they go a long way in helping us feel connected. I would encourage John and Joan to be sure that they are communicating on at least this level before they move on to addressing the deeper issues that may exist.

After reading about John and Joan's situation, Shirley wrote,

> That was the story of my life for forty-two years. During the last five years, it has really intensified; Nate retired from the Air Force and went with industry. He has been to China and Russia almost three times a month. Over the years I have had the full range of emotions: feeling neglected, wanting to divorce and find someone who really "cared more about me than his job," creating arguments to try to get my point across, ignoring him, developing my own interests, pretending I didn't care, gaining sympathy from other people for my "sad state of affairs"—and the list goes on.

From her experience, Shirley suggests that Joan start by beginning to express her thanks for what John does do—he comes home faithfully, spends Saturday nights with her, and provides for her. Since we know that John is a Powerful Choleric, we understand that he has a need to be appreciated for all the work he does. He believes he is doing what he needs to do as a husband by providing well for Joan. Men see togetherness much differently than women do; their being in the same room—or house—is often sufficient "together time" for men. In talking about her marriage, Shirley says,

> My Powerful Choleric husband, Nate, did not need to spend any time with friends or even spend Saturday night together [with me]. Being in the same room was great "togetherness" for him. Once I realized that being in the same room with him, even though we didn't converse, fulfilled his "togetherness" idea, I could relax with it.

Meanwhile Joan needs to be sure that her heart is right. Like Joan, Jo found that when her husband traveled, she had to fight resentment. Jo reports,

> Because my husband, Ray, had been bored in his prior job, I actually encouraged him to take a career advancement to North American sales manager even though it would require more travel. I put a cute and silly, or loving and sexy, card in his suitcase for him to find every time he left home. We talked nightly on the phone. But when his travel time became so extensive that it took him away from me for week-long stretches, back to back, month after month, the stress built within both of us, and our relationship became less tender and caring. I fought resentment, but I knew I had encouraged this change. I often prayed about my attitude.

If Joan attempts to address her concerns with John and she is full of anger, her attempts will backfire and may drive him away. Perhaps this is why talking has not been effective. Gaylen Larson, Ph.D., warns Joan,

> You need to understand the principle that anger feeds anger. If you approach John in an angry manner, you will feed his anger, resulting in a negative outcome. Proverbs says a soft answer turns away anger, and that an angry answer feeds anger (Proverbs 15:1). What you want to do is to dispel the anger, not feed it.

To love John extravagantly, Joan needs to be willing to make the first changes—much like the advice given to Elizabeth in the "Married From Our Dysfunctions" chapter (14). Joan can begin to make some personal changes through her time with the Lord. Without evening family responsibilities, she has plenty of time to look at her own issues. Addressing her similar concerns, Shirley says,

> Although I was deeply involved in speaking and women's ministry, the lack of togetherness began to take its toll. I could feel myself moving toward depression, so I began journaling my feelings. I recall getting up one morning at three and going downstairs to write my thoughts to God. I was very honest with Him— since God already knows my heart. I asked Him to help me understand and accept Nate for who and what he is: a good provider, a man of high integrity, a man who I know loves me (in his own way)—and to help me support him in the areas of his needs. The Lord helped me find a good Christian friend who would listen in confidence to my complaints, but would not allow me to tear Nate down or wallow in my self-pity. She listened, empathized with me, and then challenged me with ways to help understand and accept his work and his ways—to love extravagantly, though she did not use that term.
>
> Now I pray for Nate, and I encourage Joan to do the same for John. I suggest that Joan read *The Power of a Praying Wife*, by Stormie Omartian. Another wonderful book is *Personality Plus*, by Florence Littauer. Understanding the Personalities and his "work" mode versus her "friend/social" mode would be extremely helpful to Joan and John as it was for Nate and me.

Once Joan has given the Issue to God and made the mental adjustment from anger to understanding, accepting John for who he is, focusing on his good points, I encourage her to be sure that home is a place where he feels welcome and wanted.

In our marriage, I am the one who is often on the road. But as with Joan, Chuck doesn't like that I travel. However, traveling has been a part of my life for all my adult years. When I met Chuck, I was teaching seminars all over the country. I think he should be used to it after eighteen years of marriage. Instead, he likes it less and less.

However, like Joan, I am the one who was unhappy with the way things were, I was the one who wanted a change. Coming home on the plane, I often enjoy the relaxing escape of romance novels. As I read, I picture Chuck meeting me at the gate with roses in his hand. Or at least dropping what he is doing when I walk in the door to hug me, kiss me, and confirm how much he has missed me.

In reality, the plane lands, I walk alone through the terminal, get my baggage, and go to my car. I wait in line to pay for parking and drive home. Because I like to get home from a trip as soon as possible, I frequently arrive late at night rather than the next day. Chuck is often asleep when I get home. I tiptoe in, drop my bags, and undress in the dark. I crawl into bed beside him and he wiggles his toes against my leg to welcome me home. Hardly the romance novel scene I had painted in my mind.

Once I was scheduled to fly home the day after a seminar, and it happened to be our sixteenth anniversary. Since it was our anniversary, I really wanted that romance novel scene. The day before, I had arranged to have flowers sent to Chuck's office with a card that said "Happy Anniversary! Hurry home!" (I had the flowers delivered in the morning in case he forgot what day it was. They would remind him, and he'd have time to do whatever he needed to do.) I planned to arrive home before he got off work. I had time to shop for the ingredients to make a lovely dinner. I got home, did the dinner prep work, and put it all aside. In the bedroom I found something small and black hanging on our four-poster bed with an anniversary card. (He hadn't forgotten, after all.) I relaxed in a bubble bath and put my present on. I lit candles in the bedroom and put something bubbly in the silver bucket next to the bed with two crystal flutes. It was nearly time for him to get home. I crawled up on the bed and read my romance novel. I waited. The dogs barked and I heard his car door. I tucked the romance novel away and placed myself artfully across the bed. I could write my own romance novel with the results of my efforts!

Since I had sent Chuck flowers, he knew that I had not forgotten what day it was. He knew I'd be waiting, and he knew what he had waiting for me. He was excited to see me, glad I had come home. While the night left me breathless, I thought it through the next morning. That was the reaction I'd like to get every time I come home!

Romans 12:18 tells me that it is my job to "live at peace with everyone." It does not tell me to change my husband. I thought, "What could I change that would bring about the desired effect?" First, I could change my schedule so I got home before him, instead of after he was asleep. I could fix a special dinner. I could put on one of the many "little somethings" he has given me over the years, and I could place myself across the bed as if in a lingerie catalog. Yes, I could do that. My next trip I did. It worked again—even without the special day and without the flowers. My next trip I tried it again. It worked again. I had created an attitude adjustment. While he is still not crazy about my traveling, he loves my coming home. Without travel, I wouldn't be putting forth the homecoming effort. (I do not go through my "attitude adjustment" routine every time I come home—it would lose the sense of surprise that makes it special.)

While I doubt that John is expecting a romance-novel greeting, Joan can make some adjustments to be sure he feels welcome, giving him a sense of excitement and enthusiasm about coming home. On the nights that he gets home early enough, she might prepare his favorite meal and serve it in front of the fireplace. When his arrival hour is late, she could try my routine—spending time pampering herself with a bubble bath (or whatever works for her) and getting in the right frame of mind. As Shirley suggests, make his homecomings special:

> I believe that if Joan begins to accept John just as he is and lets him know that she appreciates his being such a good provider and acknowledges to him that "traveling all the time must be hard on him," and then asks what she can do to make his homecomings special, she will begin to see a difference in their relationship.

By following Shirley's advice and my example, Joan will be creating an environment that is conducive to discussing her other concerns: their limited time together and how many of her needs go unmet. Then she can ask John what his thoughts are and what he sees might take place to remedy the situation.

For example, when Jo addressed her concerns with Ray, she chose a time when they were doing something they enjoyed. She said to him, "We have such fun together. I love you and want you to be happy in your work, but I married you to share a life with you, not to live alone."

By this point, we hope John will be willing to discuss Joan's concerns and make some changes. He must recognize his role as a husband is more than just bringing home a paycheck and playing spouse for a night. Gene, who travels for his job as well, advises, "John must find balance in his schedule. If a conversation does not resolve the Issue, then they should make an appointment to visit a marriage counselor."

Jo agrees with Gene and empathizes with Joan:

> Joan has her hands full because she appears to be the one in the relationship who sees what is happening. As much as she tries to understand the pressure John is under, and how that might be a good reason to play golf with friends every Sunday, she appears to be feeling neglected. When she does try to tell John her feelings, he doesn't validate those feelings or her concerns, but merely justifies his actions. Since it is already to this point, I think Joan needs to seek a counselor or other professional person with whom she can talk. She needs to ask John to see this person with her so the third party can help John see and hear how neglected Joan feels. Joan is concerned for good reason, and to let it continue like this will only build resentment within her and dangerously cool her desire to spend future time with her husband.

Once Joan and John discuss the issues that are present in their marriage— whether on their own or with a counselor helping them—and have opened up the lines of communication, they can then address the concern Jo mentioned: spending time together.

CREATIVE TIME TOGETHER

The presenting Issue shows that Joan and John have fallen into a trap many couples face, traveling spouse or not. Their relationship has a routine and lacks excitement, variety, and a creative use of time together—which is especially important due to the limited time available. While John is working very hard and providing for Joan, the first change he must make is to draw some boundaries and make Joan a priority on the weekends—since they both have this time off.

Sometimes when I travel I am gone weekdays, other times weekends—occasionally both. When Chuck is off weekends and I am home, I make it a policy that my weekends are his. I do not make any plans until I know what he wants to do. Once in a while he wants to go for a bike ride with his friends or build something with a buddy. On those days, I do my projects. Otherwise, I do whatever he wants.

While I have been writing this book Chuck's schedule has been extremely varied. Some weeks he has been working seven days in a row. He hasn't had two days off in a row the entire time I have been writing. Last week he found out at the last minute that he would have the next day off. At first I said I could not play with him that day, as I had to write. Then I realized, what good is writing a book on marriage if my own marriage is not my priority? Fortunately I am self-employed. I put my writing aside and took the day off. We slept in—got out of bed around eleven, had a late breakfast, and went inline skating for three hours. We went to lunch around three-thirty and took a sunset motorcycle ride that evening. Chuck appreciated that I made him my priority and spent the day with him doing whatever he wanted.

John needs to do the same thing for Joan. Since his weekdays, and part of the weekend, don't involve Joan, he needs to make some sacrifices for his marriage. From his own experience with his wife and travel schedule, Gene recommends, "John must place a priority on spending time with Joan. He needs to focus more on her rather than playing golf every Sunday. John should try to consolidate as much work as possible during the week, leaving only a minimum for Saturday."

If John makes this adjustment, spending more time with Joan, they can probably reach an agreement that would allow John to golf with his buddies once or twice a month, and spend time with Joan the other Sundays.

Even if John does not change his priorities and carve out more time to spend with Joan, the time they do have needs to be more creative and stimulating for both of them. Gene says, "Rather than follow the same routine every week, they need to explore some new activities. Joan needs to arrange a Saturday evening to attend a play or a concert, visit a museum, or spend a romantic evening together at a favorite restaurant."

Chuck suggests that they take turns making the decision on how they will spend whatever time they do have together. Once the activity has been decided upon, both must agree to go for it with full enthusiasm. For example, Joan may enjoy the symphony more than John—many women do. So she might select that for their evening out. John needs to go without complaining and make the best of it. Likewise, Joan needs to go to a football game enthusiastically if that is something John might choose to do.

I enjoy going to our symphony's performances, but I especially enjoy them when they are outdoors. Chuck is okay with the symphony, but he really dislikes any activity that is indoors and likes almost anything that is outdoors. Four times a year the New Mexico Symphony plays outside at the zoo. The attire is casual and people bring a blanket or chairs and sit on the lawn with a picnic. These outdoor concerts are a good compromise for us. To make it extra special, I prepare a terrific picnic menu and pack everything. Chuck gets out the red wagon and we load it all into the car. At the zoo our little red wagon attracts a lot of admiration as Chuck pulls it to a grassy spot loaded with the chairs, blanket, picnic basket, and cooler. We agree that lying under the stars listening to Gershwin is about as perfect as a summer evening gets.

Chuck does the symphony for me. I go on motorcycle rides for him. He has a Harley Sportster. If that means anything to you, you know it is not a comfortable bike for long rides. His has a little buttonlike seat on the back fender for passengers. When we go for longer rides through the mountains to a famous motorcyclist hangout for lunch, I find myself hanging on and praying, "Oh, God, help me have a good attitude." It must have worked; now I am the one suggesting that we go on a motorcycle ride—and the restaurant has really good burgers!

We often go for hikes—picnicking at the waterfalls. Yesterday Chuck told me, "Next day off, I want to go to Santa Fe." Whenever that may be, I'll be delighted to join him. Santa Fe has great restaurants!

For Chuck's birthday this year, I wanted to do something very different. I had been on the road and was scheduled to come home in the middle of the day on his birthday. I thought about throwing a surprise party. But his Perfect Melancholy Personality doesn't go for that sort of thing. Have some friends over for dinner? But Chuck has been working such long hours, I knew he would not want to be "up" for a bunch of people, plus his birthday fell on a work night. I had to think of what would be special for *him*. I know Chuck likes picnics, and his work schedule has prevented us from having many this summer, so that is what I planned.

I had "happy birthday" flowers sent to him at work telling him to hurry home. I got home in time to prepare a lovely picnic dinner: grilled chicken Caesar salad with a croissant and a bubbly beverage, and fresh brownies for dessert. I packed it all up with our portable picnic table. A friend took me up to the top of the cliffs overlooking Albuquerque where I set up the picnic, arranging his presents around the table. I had left a card with a riddle at home for Chuck. When solved, he would know where to meet me. As soon as we saw Chuck driving toward the cliffs, my friend left. I was alone when Chuck got there. We ate dinner and watched the sunset in one direction and the lights of the city come on in the other. We had a lovely evening! We agreed that we needed to do that more often.

When John and Joan plan their special activities together, they need to take into consideration what they like to do together and individually. Perhaps Joan could learn to golf so John can still golf, but they could be together—or she could drive the cart.

To prevent falling into a rut, try one of the many books available that offer creative dates for couples. Simply entering the word *dating* on Amazon.com brought up over 1,600 books. Two I suggest are by Dave and Claudia Arp: *10 Dates to Revitalize Your Marriage* and *52 Dates for You and Your Mate*. Joan and John might want to get one of these books and spend an evening selecting a few dates that they both agree sound like fun.

Another issue of concern found in the presenting Issue is that it appears Joan and John do not have any spiritual connection. Church attendance should be one of the activities that they do together as their Christian life offers the foundation for their marriage commitment. They might seek out a church with worship services offered on Saturday night as well as Sunday. Attending on Saturday would leave Sunday morning open for their personal quality time. While this may sound somewhat heretical to some, I think God would honor the decision to encourage a healthy marital relationship.

Even after Joan and John work together to improve their communication, talk about their concerns, and spend creative time together, they might find that they are still suffering from lack of sufficient together time. In fact, once they really start to enjoy each other again, they may find that they both resent John's traveling even more. Since Joan is a schoolteacher, she may be able to join John on some of his trips during the summer. Jo traveled with Ray from time to time. She says,

> We tried to work it out so that I could go with Ray occasionally, but Ray eventually decided he missed being with me more than he enjoyed the prestigious title

and the hectic schedule it required. When an opportunity to change positions presented itself, Ray took it in order to cut back on travel time. He was highly respected in his industry, and when he answered the question about why he took a demotion in his career, he answered truthfully, "To spend less time on the road and more time with my wife. Our relationship is more important than anything." Every man hearing that has told Ray he admires him for doing it. We are thoroughly enjoying having more time together.

While all traveling men or women won't look at the situation as Ray did, they do need to value the feelings and insight of their marriage partner and respond with care and love. When Chuck and I lived in different states for five months, I drove back and forth most weekends. We tried hard to make it work. But it is very difficult to have a marriage when weekends are all you have together. Amanda said this about her long-distance marriage:

> Tony was a national sales manager. He left Monday morning and came home on Friday night—it was hard! After a year, he went to work for someone else, and we've made sure never to live like that again. It was way too hard on the relationship.

Many couples live apart long term. Others, like Amanda and Tony, make it through a few months of a temporary situation. Whichever your case, I hope the insights offered here will help you love each other extravagantly—to give, not to get.

Interaction

1. The couple needs to create a balance sheet on John's job to determine if it is worth the strain on the marriage. In separate columns, they should list the costs and benefits of the current job. This will help them see in black and white whether or not John should stay in this job.

2. Each spouse should ask him or herself, "If things remain exactly the same, how long do I think I can hang in there?" Then share the responses. This is an indicator of how critical the situation is and how urgent the need for change. Different solutions to the Issue require more time to complete than others. When time is short, bold action is required.

3. Depending on the answers to the previous exercises, begin to look for avenues for change. For example, if both agree that a job change is not needed, what changes can be made in the weekend routine? List specific variations and select one

for each upcoming weekend. Even if a job change is agreed upon, it may take months to implement. Therefore, a change in the weekend routine may still be needed.

4. Because of the minimal time this couple has together, they need to maximize the time that they do have. Schedule time weekly—about an hour—to do the couple's communication exercise (see appendix D). It will be especially valuable to this situation.

Bet the Farm

Job Loss, Security, Life Direction

The Issue

*I*t was the second marriage for both Rich and Pat. If their expectations for their first marriage had been high, now they had bet the farm. They were older, more mature; the children from their first marriages were grown and off on their own. They had promised to love each other's offspring, make them welcome in their new home, and never accuse the children's other parent of wrong. They were aware that their divorces had forced their children into new, strange, and frightening circumstances.

It would be just the two of them working on their lives together, going forward with their hopes and dreams. They knew something of their mistakes, were somewhat aware of their shortcomings, and had resolved that nothing would destroy what they had found together. They had moved to Southern California to rebuild their lives. They left everything behind to start anew. Knowing that they needed something "greater than themselves," they had committed their lives to the Lord and found a church for worship that was ideal. There they had "family," felt nourished, and made friends. It seemed everything was in place—at least for a while.

Both Rich and Pat were professionals. Pat was an editor for a major magazine and Rich was an insurance executive. Their careers were on track, money was not a problem—they were secure in their future, in one another, and in the Lord.

Then recently there was a coup in Rich's organization, and he, along with the CEO and other top executives, were thrown out. Rich has a wide range of experience and thought that getting another position would be no problem—even if it took a while. He hadn't anticipated that his age, now fifty-five, would make it difficult. He hadn't acknowledged that the business world had become a "younger place." In the months since his job loss, no career opportunities have come. Rich has tired of being "over-qualified." He is angry and scared from the inside out. Nothing in his life has any of the familiar signposts. The world has become a strange and frightening place.

Rich is beginning to realize that he has always staked his life on his abilities; his career, position, power, and influence defined him, gave him his identity and respectability. He has competed in the corporate marketplace, provided for his family, and seen to it that Pat never endured what he witnessed his parents go through—until now. It seems that his abilities no longer count.

While Rich has been struggling, Pat's magazine position has suddenly come to an abrupt end. Although she has been a career person, she always thought there would be a husband who would take care of her and see to her needs. After all, hadn't her dad done that?

With neither of them bringing in any income, they have resorted to selling off property and investments—netting far less than their original value, thus hastening more and more sell-off. Now there is nothing left.

Desperate, Rich has taken a job in a discount warehouse. The pay is a far cry from what he has known and had assumed would always be there.

Rich seems to be unable to talk with Pat about any of their circumstances or his fear and shame over this turn of events in their lives. When Pat tries to talk about what is happening to them, Rich cannot. When Pat insists, Rich becomes angry and shuts her out. Pat feels isolated, confused, and sick at heart over the situation. But even more over the fact that she and Rich don't seem to be partners any longer. She finds she distances herself from her husband and seeks to find her own way in activities that further separate them.

Insights

Many of us in a modern marriage can relate to Rich and Pat's story. Often couples seem to do well when life is cruising along, but when the difficulties crash upon them, underlying issues come to the surface. With the instability of today's job market, men and women who thought their career path was firm find themselves in a position similar to Rich and Pat's. To ensure that the Insight offered here will be helpful to many couples, we will look primarily at security and life direction.

SECURITY

Rich's predicament is very typical of men today, though some women face it too, whose security and worth is centered in their profession. However, as a Christian, Rich needs to find his value in his life in Christ—as work does not define the believer. Gaylen Larson, Ph.D., adds, "[One must] find and practice his giftedness as defined in 1 Corinthians 12."

Charles understands how Rich feels. Charles and his wife, Karen, faced similar circumstances when a company reshuffle caused him to lose his position as a CFO in a major insurance company at fifty-nine. Charles says of that time in his life:

> My greatest fear was that I could no longer depend on myself. Hard work and experience now made no difference. Success and accomplishment eluded me. I had "worshiped" at those altars all my life. It was all I knew; it was what made me worthy.

When Charles' self worth was in question, he pulled away from Karen and isolated himself, taking his anger at the world out on her. Many times Karen found herself reminding Charles that she was not the enemy. As Charles pushed her away, she had to do things on her own. She took up hiking and camping. She got some counsel, and she grew—all the while being patient with Charles as he dealt with his fears. During this time Charles took a job as a night manager at a gas station where he had previously been a customer. His time of transition included driving a laundry truck, selling shoes, and managing the shoe department in a clothing store.

As Karen grew, Charles realized that if he wanted to keep up with her, he needed to make some changes as well. Finally he turned to Christian counseling and got involved in a men's Bible study. Charles says,

> It wasn't long before I saw that my worth was caught up in my corporate image. It was time to lean on the Lord as never before. Now it seemed the Lord was instructing me that obedience to His directives was my business; the outcome of my endeavors was His. He would teach me that being smart, having power, prestige, and position had kept me from Him. He showed me that He would allow hurt and pain, failure and guilt, confusion and remorse to attack me so that finally there would be no place for me to go but to Him.

Chuck and I faced something similar as well. Economics in the health care profession caused Chuck to take a job in sales much below his expectations and education. While waiting for customers at the Jaguar dealer, he had time to read through the entire Bible. In doing so, God showed him that work is just work. The apostle Paul was a tentmaker—though his education and position as a Pharisee would indicate that he could have had a much more prestigious position. Prior to his encounter with Christ, we can assume that Paul held an authoritative post within the Jewish community. Yet the Bible does not talk much about Paul's profession, but more about his actions and how he changed the world after his conversion. The *Life Application Bible*'s Personality Profile says, "No person, apart from Jesus himself, shaped the history of Christianity like the apostle Paul."[1]

Charles and Chuck were Christians when life dealt them a hard blow. For both of them, it was in that down time that their relationship with Christ grew to a new level, to a place where they could view their job as just that—a job, like tentmaking. It does not define who they are.

While it is easier said than done, the first step Chuck advises Rich to take is to adjust his thinking about his worthiness. His job at the discount warehouse is just a job, a way to bring in some income, but it does not determine who he is. Gaylen Larson sees that Rich is struggling with self-esteem issues from which he feels as if he will never recover. As a result, Dr. Larson says,

> Because men define their worth by what they do, it would be important for Pat to go overboard in complimenting him. It may also help if he would teach a class at church or be involved in some leadership. This will help him feel better about himself.

Kurt and Stephanie have been leading marriage enrichment classes for four years; they encourage Rich to get involved in a small group, as Charles did. They say, "We have found small groups are a great way to find support, love, and friendship. With a group that is based on Christ, healing will take place."

Once Rich reaches this place and allows his relationship with Christ to take on a deeper meaning in his life, he can then begin to see his marriage as a three-way relationship between Pat, God, and himself. Charles tells of this time in his life:

> God taught me that my relationship with Karen was a direct barometer of how my relationship was with Him. Now I marvel at what the Lord has given us in our marriage. It is simply sweet. It is far beyond what I had thought would be possible for us, or for any marriage. As it is in all things, this marriage is His, not mine, not Karen's—but I am sure glad I am one of the participants!

Stephanie agrees:

> From my study of Scripture and Jesus' saying "I have come to heal the sick," it has become more and more apparent to me just what He meant by that statement. Marriage with Jesus will not be trouble free, but it will survive. Marriages without

Christ barely have a chance on this earth—even if things look great on the outside, they may be falling apart on the inside. We have learned the importance of the unity created when Christ becomes a part of the marriage.

Once Rich is able to make this shift in his thinking and his relationship with Christ, Chuck advises that he and Pat need to begin to build communication and open up to their true feelings. Maxine Marsolini, author of *Blended Families*, offers Rich and Pat this counsel:

> When life throws you a curve ball, and you should expect it will once in a while, it would be best to cleave together in prayer and goal attainment. Rich and Pat seem to have tied their sense of worth to their pocketbook and not to their core personhood set forth by their creator. Both are bright and capable in their own right, but until they can talk about their true feelings it will be difficult to overcome the shame that accompanies their unmet expectations. Humility is often a hard ball to grasp, yet is the very core element of Christianity and marital bliss.

From her own similar experience, Sherrie suggests that Pat create an environment that will disarm Rich's aversion to discuss their situation:

> I would encourage Pat to request that she and Rich join one another in prayer each day, even if it is just for a minute and regarding nothing seemingly significant. It is amazing the closeness that is fostered when a couple begins to pray together on a regular basis. This gets them comfortable with one another in the presence of the One with the answers. It also allows for "comfortable" vulnerability over time.

For Charles and Karen, prayer was an important part of the restoration of their relationship as well. Charles reflects,

> We began to pray together each morning—walking and talking. Then we came together to discuss finances, future goals, and decisions that would affect our children.

As Charles was rediscovering himself in Christ, he was able to talk to Karen about what he was learning. Karen welcomed his conversations and encouraged him. Eventually they recommitted themselves to the Lord, to each other, and to their family.

The scenario mentions that Pat expected that while she planned to work, she also thought she would have a husband who would be there to take care of her. As discussed in the "Career Chaos" chapter (5), the reality today is that Pat needs to let go of that expectation. Jobs are no longer secure, and a couple needs to work together. This is one of the ways that the love extravagantly concept can be put into practice: Pat needs to let go of her expectations and anger toward Rich for not being there for her in her time of need—"not to get but to give." Stephanie advises,

> True love, extravagant love, is helping each other, supporting each other, and esteeming the other as better than yourself.

LIFE DIRECTION

Help on attitude adjustment came for Chuck in some entertaining armchair travel books by Peter Mayle: *A Year in Provence, Toujours Provence,* and *Encore Provence*. In these books, Mayle introduces a French habit he calls the "classic Gaelic shrug," a physical expression that means so much more. He describes it this way:

> A certain amount of limbering-up is required before any major body parts are brought into action, and your first moves should be nothing more than a frown and a slight sideways tilt of the head. These indicate that you cannot believe the foolishness, the impertinence, or the plain dumb ignorance of what the Parisian has just said to you. There is a short period of silence before the Parisian tries again, repeating this remark and looking at you with some degree of irritation. Maybe he thinks you're deaf, or Belgian, and therefore confused by his sophisticated accent. Whatever he feels, you now have his complete attention. This is the moment to demolish him and his nonsense with a flowing, unhurried series of movements as the full shrug is unfurled.
>
> Step One: The jaw is pushed out as the mouth is turned down.
>
> Step Two: The eyebrows are fully cocked and the head comes forward.
>
> Step Three: The shoulders are raised to earlobe level, the elbows tucked in to the side, the hands fanning out with palms facing upward.
>
> Step Four (optional): You allow a short, infinitely dismissive sound—something between flatulence and a sigh—to escape from your lips before letting the shoulders return to a resting position.
>
> It might almost be a yoga exercise, and I must have seen it hundreds of times. It can be used to signify disagreement, disapproval, resignation, or contempt, and it effectively terminates any discussion. As far as I know, there is no counter-shrug or satisfactory answering gesture. For these reasons, it is an invaluable gesture for anyone like myself whose command of the French language is far from perfect. A well-timed shrug speaks volumes.[2]

With the body language of the shrug, the person says, "Oh well, life goes on." Chuck suggests that Rich practice this cognitive process by pairing the physical action—palms turned out, elbows tucked in, corners of the mouth turned down, with the mental letting go/letting God idea. Chuck has been working on making this behavior modification in his own life. Rather than getting upset or being too hard on himself, Chuck is learning to shrug. Sometimes he will just look at me and say, "Shrug." He is learning to let go and would advise Rich to do the same.

Chuck asks Rich to consider, "Is God preparing both of you for something new? Should you start a business or ministry together? Do something with e-commerce or go back to school?" Along the same lines, Sherrie suggests that Rich capitalize on his experience by "mining" the treasures. She encourages Rich and Pat to

> Look at writing an article in a business magazine as an option, a Web site support group for displaced executives, a how-to booklet on avoiding the unexpected pitfalls in the business world, and the like. Often community colleges hire executives and other experts to teach business classes at night. If Rich was to find some outlet for giving of himself—possibly in a mentorship capacity to a younger man, volunteer a few hours a month in an area of his interests—it would help curb self-pity and go far toward gaining a new healthier view of himself. When people start to feel better about themselves, it seems that the rest of life tends to line up better and gravitate toward more positive experiences.

Many people have chosen to leave the corporate rat race and make a different life for themselves. In Rich and Pat's case, perhaps God has made the choice for them. Shrug—and move on. In reading about Rich and Pat, Jan and Carl responded by saying,

> Our situation is mildly similar, except that we both chose to leave the corporate world—which meant severe downsizing and adapting a mindset of simplifying life so we had more time to pursue our passions and serve the Lord. . . . It has brought on struggles for which we were not prepared, and we are constantly re-examining our priorities, life mission, and how we define ourselves. As two separate people bringing in two paychecks, it is easy to be independent, but downsizing forces interdependence and sacrifice, needs versus wants, and a complete change in lifestyle.

While the practical reality was far more complicated than the dream of carrying it out, Jan and Carl report that they would not trade their situation for the way it was. From their experience, they offer Rich and Pat hope:

Rich and Pat need to see the blessing in being free of the corporate jungle and that God's hand is in it. The warehouse job is only a stopgap measure to bring in some groceries. Both should find out what God is calling them to do and do it—no matter what the salary. Sell the big house, if they have one, and live in what they can afford. They are both healthy and still young; there is no reason for poverty. Without the trappings, they will find greater meaning in life!

Interaction

1. In a communication exercise format (see appendix D), each spouse should talk through his and her fears with one another. In a written format, list the worst-case scenario for the coming months. What is the worst that could happen? Flip the paper over (indicating two sides of the coin) and write out the best-case scenario, all the good that could come in spite of financial losses. This exercise should draw the husband and wife together. Additionally, after completing the assignment, the couple would see that much of the situation is under their control. They have a choice whether they make the best or the worst of these circumstances. They can distance themselves from each other and from God, living in fear. Or they can take this time to draw closer to each other, to God, walking in faith and embarking on a new adventure.

2. It is a mistake for people to identify themselves strictly by their current job. Individually the spouses should write out their self-identity, listing all the things that make up who they are—in light of what they would want their grandchildren to remember about them. This will help each to remove their focus from the unimportant, their profession, and on to what is enduring.

"So all their work is useless, like chasing the wind" (Ecclesiastes 2:26b).

3. Set common and personal goals for growth. For example, the couple might decide to spend one hour a day in Bible study; they might choose to work on their physical health by spending time in exercise together or learning to cook. This shift in their career focus will allow them more time for personal growth. Working toward achieving these goals will keep the couple from dwelling on the negative while making good use of the available time.

4. Spouses, independently, should write out their expectations of the other during this trying time. Then come together and discuss them, agreeing upon changes that each is willing to make. Some expectations may prove to be valid; others will need to be thrown out once they are verbalized. When expectations are clear and agreed upon, resentment, hostility, and anger toward each other will be minimized.

Chapter FOUR

Sacrificed Her Career

Caregiving, Personal Fulfillment, Career Options

The Issue

*T*roy was a high-powered salesman, flying half a million miles a year—gathering up frequent flyer tickets the way some people collect grocery coupons. A gregarious Powerful Choleric with some Perfect Melancholy, Troy had a massive stroke six and a half years ago. He was fifty-six. Annette, his Popular Sanguine/Powerful Choleric wife, was forty-six. While originally completely debilitated, Troy has progressed from a wheelchair to a cane, and now to walking—although his left leg still drags a bit. Together Troy and Annette have worked their way back to a halfway "normal" life.

The first three years after Troy's stroke, Annette was his primary caregiver. She quit her job because she couldn't leave him long enough to go to work. The stroke caused him to do things that were unsafe—he'd leave the water running or the gas stove on. But he finally got beyond that, began to drive, and now pretty much functions as he had before. He has lost the use of his left arm, but manages to compensate.

Around year four, people began to ask Annette why she didn't get a job. With neither of them working, their income went from over $100,000 a year to less than $35,000 from disability insurance. They could use an extra income. Annette's self-image began to suffer as they continued living on the disability payments, and she missed the intellectual stimulation her job had provided.

One of the things that attracted Annette to Troy was the power that came from his position. He was strong and together they had an enviable lifestyle. Now after six and a half years of disability, Troy no longer has the same magnetism he once did. While Annette has stood by his side and supported him through the difficulties, she is concerned about going back into the work force. Her effervescent nature has always attracted men, especially those who want to take care of her. Annette feels empty. She is afraid if a man paid any attention to her, it would be too great a temptation—she might up and run away! However, she loves her husband and as a Christian feels she should not put herself in what could be a compromising position. So she's remained at home—waiting for the Lord to show her a better idea.

The stroke and its aftermath created an extreme shift in the marriage—Annette and Troy need a new equilibrium. Annette wants to continue to grow. Her husband now looks old to her and she still feels young! She believes she sacrificed her career to save her marriage. However, Annette now is in a place where she can do something that uses her skills and abilities while giving her the mental and emotional stimulation she longs for.

Insights

While Troy and Annette's situation presents her need for a job and her fear of temptation as primary concerns, we see a bigger issue. This is common to many women, no matter how healthy their husbands may be: expecting her husband to fulfill all of her needs and interests. If Annette addresses this first, her career options and the temptation they provide will be less of a worry.

PERSONAL FULFILLMENT

Annette's Personality is the combination of the Popular Sanguine/Powerful Choleric. This tells us she likes lots of activity and stimulation. Additionally, we know that Annette is ten years younger than Troy. So while Troy is ready to slow down and retire—possibly even if he had no disability—Annette still desires more activity.

Annette is to be commended for honoring her marriage vows and sticking with Troy through the past six years. Being a caregiver is not a position that her Personality type would naturally gravitate toward. Now, however, Annette says that she is running on empty. This is natural in her place. For over six years she has been doing nothing that fills her or stimulates her. Her whole life has been focused around her husband and caring for him—she has been giving extravagant love.

Fortunately for Annette, she now can make some changes. Unlike a terminally or chronically ill person, Troy no longer needs constant care. If your situation today is that of being a caregiver, either long term or temporary, you need something that will offer you emotional and spiritual nourishment to fill you up—or like Annette, you will find that you are running on empty.

As I talk to women around the country I find that many of them expect their husband to fulfill all their needs: physical, emotional, and spiritual. If he isn't their provider, best friend, spiritual leader, and companion in shared activities they feel disappointed and cheated. I believe it is unreasonable to expect any one human being to meet all our needs. In her book *The Power of Femininity*, Michelle McKinney Hammond says,

> We will strive, weep and deprive ourselves of opportunities to live a full life if we put our hope in a person to fulfill our expectations.[1]

First, many of our needs can only be met through an ongoing and active relationship with our Lord Jesus Christ. So I would ask Annette about her spiritual walk. Is she in a women's Bible study group, one that offers her spiritual food and fellowship? Because the fellowship aspect is so important for Annette as she finds a new equilibrium in her marriage, I believe a group study is a vital link for her. She could read the Bible or use a study guide on her own. Both of these activities would be beneficial, but a group study also will offer her much-needed social interaction. Annette may have to visit several different groups before she finds one that meets her personal needs.

To find out about Bible study groups in her area, she might start with the women's ministries in her church, then call some of the major churches near her home, or check with the local Christian bookstore. Christian bookstores often know of Bible study groups because they have ordered supplies for them or because they have postings of Christian activities. Another option is to look in the local newspaper's religion section (usually on Saturday) that lists events taking place within the community.

In addition, Annette and Troy should consider studying the Bible together— either a couples' group study or just the two of them. Maxine Marsolini, author of *Blended Families*, suggests that they participate in an ongoing couples' Bible study. She recommends a study called *Becoming One* by Don Meridith. Maxine says,

> [*Becoming One*] is a great study to do because it moves life's trials away from selfish feelings into an enjoyable and focused Extravagant Love commitment.

Attending a group study will help Annette fill both her spiritual and social needs. As a Popular Sanguine, her need for friendship cannot be ignored. Consequently I encourage Annette to seek other forms of social activity with female friends as well. Is there a physical activity she enjoys or has enjoyed in the past? In my area, the local bike store hosts a women's ride every Wednesday evening. I have enjoyed joining them occasionally for a casual ride along the river. Many gyms host aerobics classes or other group activities that would provide Annette with a forum for meeting women her age and with similar interests. Taking a class through the community college or other adult education programs would be another option. Annette needs to develop a social network of friends who can encourage her and lift her up. After being Troy's caretaker for six years, Annette may find many of her former friends have moved on. Additionally, her previous social network was probably largely related to her work. She needs to get out and make new friends.

Another way Annette can fill her emotional tank and prevent the running-on-empty feeling is with activities she enjoys. If these activities are things she once did with Troy and he is no longer able to do them or isn't interested in doing them, she can explore other avenues. For example, I like to sail. Chuck does not enjoy it the same way I do. He would rather ride his bike. Since sailing is not something I can easily do all by myself, I gave it up for a while. I found that I was harboring resentment toward Chuck because he did not join in this activity with me. Then I realized it is unrealistic to expect Chuck to share every activity with me or for me to expect Chuck to meet 100 percent of my needs. One day our newspaper had a feature on a local sailing club that holds races on the lakes here in New Mexico. I joined. I love the feeling of standing on the bow with the wind in my hair, the sun on my face, and the splash of refreshing water cooling me off. While I have to drive three hours each way to get to a lake, the drive seems like nothing compared to the satisfaction I receive from the activity.

These three areas—spiritual walk, friends, and satisfying activities—will nourish Annette's soul and help her feel fulfilled. For her Personality, these are important. If she feels strengthened and stimulated with healthy activities, the temptation to stray will be lessened.

While this prescription will help Annette, or anyone else in a care-giving situation, it will do little to restore her marriage's vitality. Since Troy is now capable of at least a somewhat normal life, they need to explore things they can do together. Helen says of Annette and Troy's situation,

Oh, my heart goes out to Annette. I know firsthand how a serious illness or injury can affect a marriage. I, too, am disabled. I had an accident. Annette needs to remember that her husband is still the same man she loved and married. While it is a challenge, she can still have a glorious and exciting marriage. If she and her husband can learn to focus on doing everything they can think to do to court and encourage each other, her life will be sweet. Now is the time to test those vows they repeated when they were married. They've made it through the worst part. They can now start rebuilding what was lost. God promises that he will restore the years the locusts have eaten (Joel 2:25). An affair with another man can't compare with the joy she can find right in her own marriage if she will seek ways to build her husband up. If she will crown him her king, he in turn will treat her as his queen. What a payoff! I've experienced restoration in my marriage and it is marvelous.

In an effort to rebuild what was lost, Annette and Troy might try traveling together. Every few months they could plan a special weekend away at a bed and breakfast. They might take a photography class or a gourmet cooking class together. Whatever their interests or level of physical activity, they need to do things together that they can both enjoy. For Annette, loving Troy extravagantly may mean being willing to adjust her faster pace to his new lower-key pace. In their new place of equilibrium, the things they did together formerly may no longer be possible. Rather than mourn that loss, they can celebrate what they can still do together.

As Annette and Troy work to rebuild their life and their relationship, they should look at a couple of additional areas. Melanie Wilson, Ph.D., is concerned that Annette will act irresponsibly if she does not find an outlet for her anger and grief. Dr. Wilson asks,

Has she expressed her anger through journaling, prayer, or to her husband? Although she has willingly submitted her own needs to care for her husband (and this is to be praised), she must have some feelings of anger, disappointment, and grief. If she has not worked through these feelings and expressed them openly, trouble could still be brewing. Sharing her anger and grief with her husband and directing it at the stroke (rather than at him), can be healing and restorative. Doing something as simple as writing down the things that the stroke took away from them can be a wonderful exercise. Only when the anger and grief have been expressed can the couple focus on the blessings they still share and the strengths they can capitalize on in the future.

"I agree with Melanie," says Jo.

I, too, am disabled. I was married for eight years before being diagnosed with multiple sclerosis during my husband's first year in seminary. We wanted to trust God with the MS, and since we were already in part-time ministry, we immediately became visible examples to others. From the beginning of dealing with the disease, I poured out my fears and struggles to God in my prayer journal. I remember discussing my Scripture search regarding healing with my husband as we prayed for that very thing and did not receive the answer we desired.

God's answer has been, "I will be with you in the midst of MS," and He has done that very thing for over twenty-three years. I learned to thank Him while dealing with it (1 Thessalonians 5:18) and thank Him for what He could do in and through it (Ephesians 5:20). Praising God for who He is, not what He could do for me became crucial for my spiritual growth (Psalm 92:1–2; 2 Corinthians 1:3).

Five years after the diagnosis, my husband, who was a full-time pastor and seminary Ph.D. student, began an affair with a girlfriend of mine. From things my husband said about MS during that time, it seemed obvious to me—and others—that he had become bitter and had not dealt with his anger at God, or me, for having MS and for dealing with it so well. His affair lasted over a year and nearly devastated me. Had I not continued clinging to God, I shudder to think what would have become of me. Just as Helen said, an affair does not satisfy. My husband left the pastorate, his doctoral studies, and me, then filed for a divorce I didn't want—we had been married by then for fifteen years. A year later, he called me. He told me he was sorry for having nearly destroyed me and that he was sorry for dissolving our marriage; however, he did not want to work on it again.

By not dealing with his emotional and spiritual struggles, my husband had let himself see only the MS instead of me. He resented the way our life changed rather than choosing to look for things we could do together, as I was constantly trying to do.

Four years later a wonderful man took the risk of marrying me and MS. We have had thirteen years of health challenges, ensuing spiritual and emotional growth, and more fun together than some couples ever have! We tandem because I can't ride a bike alone. We ski—I use helps designed for the disabled. We enjoy traveling and sightseeing, eating out, serving the Lord, Bible study, and worship. We enjoy sitting side-by-side knowing we share a deep love born out of adversity. But Ray also has his own hobbies and interests, something Annette really needs to work on.

Jo is a speaker, singer, and writer. She definitely hasn't let self-pity get the best of her.

While the presenting problem deals with Annette, Chuck has concern for Troy. Chuck would counsel Troy:

Stretch yourself, get away from being defined by your disability and redefine yourself with your abilities. I encourage you to connect with other men through work, church, or organizations focused on helping stroke survivors. You need to be as self-sufficient as possible, allowing Christian brothers to help when needed. This will help you to see Annette as your wife and lover rather than your nurse-maid. Expecting her to do both puts her in a difficult position.

Gaylen Larson, Ph.D., agrees that Troy needs to do something for himself and the relationship: "I suggest that Troy and Annette get involved in a small group Bible study for couples. He needs to see what he can do to win Annette back and revitalize their relationship."

CAREER OPTIONS

From Annette's comments we get the idea that her interest in returning to the work force is more from a need for stimulation rather than for money. Yes, the additional income would be beneficial, but not required. Therefore, Annette has some freedom in her occupational choices.

Victoria Jackson, LCSW, suggests that Annette create some type of entrepre-neurial home business that would allow her to bring in some income, have intellec-tual stimulation, and still be at home much of the time. She says,

> Depending on what common interests the couple had prior to the disability, they could consider a business that might entail both of them. She could even write and present workshops through the local hospital about the shift in a relationship that comes when one spouse has an illness or accident. Think creatively, talk to other couples in similar predicaments, ask the Lord for ideas, and review entre-preneurial and women's magazines for motivational stories that tell of other women's adversities and how they overcame them.

I couldn't agree more with Victoria's comments. I am a big proponent of women-owned businesses, especially those that are entrepreneurial or home-based in nature. "Celebrate Your Passions," the last chapter in my book *You've Got What it Takes*, would be an excellent resource for Annette or anyone in her position. Additionally, a home-based business would remove Annette's concerns about temp-tation and infidelity. However, Chuck comments,

> There is temptation everywhere. Rather than remove herself from any possibility of it, Annette will do better to first focus on filling that emptiness she refers to and building up her relationship with Troy.

Allison found herself in a similar position to Annette's, after her husband,

Kevin, was attacked on their ranch by a twelve-hundred-pound bull. Kevin's leg was barely saved. After five surgeries and three weeks in the hospital, he was sent home with ten pounds of metal in his leg. Like Annette, Allison is Popular Sanguine/Powerful Choleric and has little patience for nursing, but that is exactly what she did. While she preferred to go back to work, Kevin's dependence on her for everything from showering, to dressing, to using the bathroom, kept her home. Their lack of disability insurance and Kevin's inability to work forced them to sell some of their cattle and land to survive. After sixteen long months, Kevin was able to walk, and work, again. His injury caused both of them to reevaluate their lives, resulting in Allison's return to her love of writing. Now she is working on her book *God Allows U-Turns*, and is represented by a well-respected literary agent. Allison changed from working with her husband in his real estate business to living her dream. She encourages Annette to do the same:

> Look at what you have always wanted to do and take this opportunity to try something new! Kevin and I have a new equilibrium. Work no longer controls our lives. God has blessed us both with good health, a growing ministry, and a new understanding of our personalities as they relate to every area of our lives. We continue to grow as individuals as well as growing as a couple with our focus on doing God's will as the foundation of our life together.

All marriages face shifts at one time or another. Many of us face health or career challenges. By being willing to love extravagantly, to give, not to get, Annette and Troy—or you and your spouse—can find a new equilibrium that works for them, their interests, and their unique situation.

Interaction

1. The wife needs to develop interests that will bring personal fulfillment. She might join a Bible study, take a craft or cooking class, or participate in another activity where she will reconnect with women with similar interests. As her personal life is nourished, the temptation of other men will be minimized.

2. The wife needs to begin to rebuild her professional life. Start by brainstorming career options that will provide mental stimulation. Include the potential risks she feels are present in each one. A viable option might be developing a business with her husband. (See chapter 6 in *You've Got What It Takes*.)

3. The husband must identify a Christian friend to whom he can be accountable. This person will agree to be his coach, making him stretch to expand his world: someone who will get him moving when he is feeling sorry for himself and

applaud him when he has achieved a new goal.

4. The husband needs to identify ten new activities or resources to expand his life. These might be written on a dry-erase board, where they can be kept in view and changed as needed. One of them might be to link up with (or create, if needed) a support group for stroke victims. Another might be an athletic endeavor; rather than playing golf with the heavy hitters, he might go to the driving range. He might also cultivate friendships with men with similar disabilities. Using a calendar, begin scheduling two new activities a week for four consecutive weeks.

5. The husband needs to prepare a talking paper that he will later present to the wife. In developing this outline of what he will say to his wife face-to-face, he will express his appreciation for the love and care that she has provided during this medical crisis. At the end he will emphasize that he is improving daily and that as he progresses she is free to begin rebuilding her life, independent of caring for him. This will give her validation for her sacrifice while giving her permission and encouragement to expand her life. Once he has delineated the points he wants to share with his wife, perhaps reviewing them with his accountability partner, he needs to share his feelings with her.

6. Together husband and wife need to discuss their changing expectations of each other as the relationship takes on a new equilibrium. This should be done on a weekly basis during this period of transition.

Career Chaos

Security, Depression

The Issue

*C*hristine and Steve have been married for thirteen years. It is Steve's second marriage, but Christine's first. They are compatible in many ways and have similar Personalities, but in different proportions. He is Powerful Choleric with some Popular Sanguine while Christine is Perfect Melancholy first with a secondary of Powerful Choleric. While they complement each other, Christine is bewildered at how different they are in one big area: the management of their careers. Christine's path has been fairly smooth and steady; Steve's career is extremely chaotic. She absolutely loves what she does and her career has fallen into place very nicely. Steve gets depressed about his business failures.

Steve has had countless jobs in the past thirteen years. He is a salesperson, and he says it's really hard to find good sales jobs in which you can actually make a living. At the same time, he is a big dreamer with an entrepreneurial spirit. He has tried his hand at numerous ventures, but none have lasted. Sometimes he has launched out on his own, other times with a partner. Sometimes he has made a little money; usually he has gotten them deeply into debt. Whenever a business venture fails, he goes to work for some company as a salesperson. Christine is always relieved when he has a steady paycheck coming in again. But it never lasts for long because he always has his eye open for a "better opportunity"—whether that means another job or an entrepreneurial venture. Earlier this year he tried his hand at day trading, believing that to be a relatively easy business he could develop on his own. It wasn't. Again, Steve lost money.

Christine doesn't want Steve to lose his optimism and confidence about finding an "ideal" business situation. However, it wears her out just watching him! The lack of stability is nerve-racking. Steve says, "There's no guarantee of stability even if you've worked for a company for twenty years." Christine thinks, "That may be true, but we'll never know it from firsthand experience!"

She has accepted that Steve is created differently than she is and that he will probably always continue searching for "greener grass" in his career. But she struggles to cope with the constant changes and the lack of security. She has difficulty maintaining the trust and respect a wife desires to have for her husband while keeping a nonjudgmental attitude.

Insights

With the information given about Steve and Christine, I have chosen to focus on two of their problems that are apt to be most like those you may be facing: security and depression. Christine has taken a big step in accepting that, after a thirteen-year history, Steve will probably always make frequent job changes. While she can accept this intellectually, it is harder to deal with on an emotional level. As she has said, she still struggles with the "constant changes and lack of security."

SECURITY

Licensed clinical social worker Victoria Jackson agrees that Christine is wise in realizing that she cannot change Steve, but encourages Christine to make some changes in her attitude and behaviors. On a practical level, Victoria suggests that since Christine's employment is solid and stable, they should consider putting aside a nest egg to cushion the financial reverses caused by her husband's uncertain career path. Additionally, she'd advise Christine and Steve to set specific financial goals, possibly even hiring a financial planner to help them communicate their desires about what they expect from each other in matters of finance and security in their relationship. This will give Christine more security and allow her to be less judgmental of Steve's frequent job changes. Victoria believes that when Steve sees this change in Christine, he may be less defensive and resistant. Therefore, he may be more willing to take a look at what is happening with him. Victoria says, "It's my guess that part of his behavior could be childlike: 'You can't make me be responsible and predictable like you.'"

This type of response would also be typical of his Personality.

Kim offers some spiritual encouragement to Christine, saying,

I know what you are feeling because I have been in your shoes. I had to realize that ultimately God is the provider for our family, and He's always watching out for us. God must be your security, no matter what Steve's job situation might be. Read the many Scriptures that teach about God's faithful provision for all our needs (not luxuries!) and let go of the worry over the constant changes and lack of security.

Christine might want to write some of the verses addressing security on index cards and tape them to her bathroom mirror, the refrigerator, or the dashboard of her car—where she can easily see them throughout her day. A few of the verses she might start with are:

So my counsel is: Don't worry about things—food, drink, and clothes. For you already have life and a body—and they are far more important than what to eat and wear are. Look at the birds! They don't worry about what to eat—they don't need to sow or reap or store up food—for your heavenly Father feeds them. And you are far more valuable to him than they are (Matthew 6:25–26 TLB).

All who listen to me shall live in peace and safety, unafraid (Proverbs 1:33 TLB).

In dealing with her husband's job changes, Kim had to realize that times have changed. Even if her husband worked for a company for twenty years, there is no guarantee of security. People get laid off from seemingly secure jobs every day. Victoria Jackson agrees. She says,

In the 21st century, the job market is no longer the stable, predictable environment in which baby boomers grew up. The 30-year-job-with-the-gold-watch-as-a-retirement-gift kind of situation is no more.

Additionally, Steve and Christine's Personalities aggravate the situation. As a Perfect Melancholy, security and stability are very important to Christine. She has managed her professional life so that it provides her with the consistency she needs. In her childhood home, her father probably provided for the family, and she entered into her marriage believing that Steve would do the same for her. On the other hand, Steve has a built-in desire for change. He likes a challenge and is generally resilient to setbacks. He has repeatedly picked himself up, dusted himself off, and started over again—facing the world with the confidence typical of a Powerful Choleric with some Popular Sanguine. However, these very strengths have become weaknesses in his relationship with Christine.

When Kim looked at her husband's Personality, she had to believe that God created her husband as he is—bold entrepreneurial spirit and all. She exhorts Christine from her own experience:

> The fact that many more people *fail* at attempting such ventures than succeed is quite beside the point to the bold men we're married to. But that's because our men have a hard time learning from others. They are much more inclined to learn by charting their own course and *doing* things on their own, *including making their own mistakes.* Keep in mind that this concept has been ingrained in our men by their fathers, and society as a whole. It's called rugged individualism, where legendary men throughout the ages have pulled themselves up by their own boot-straps and against all odds conquered some seemingly impossible feat. Men love the scenario when it is the bottom of the ninth, two outs, nobody on base, and the team needs a miraculous home run to win the big game.

While Steve does have that need for change, that sense that he can "win the big game," Christine's inherent need for security must be addressed as well. Chuck suggests that Steve and Christine discuss Steve's next direction. Together they need to establish agreeable limits on Steve's ventures to reduce risks, to commit to a specific period of time on a job and not leave despite an opportunity that might appear more interesting, challenging, or profitable than his current position. Kim asked,

> But what about instances of *seriously* misguided intentions that you are certain will lead to catastrophe? How do you take a stand about an issue with an ambitious husband who doesn't listen very well to what you say?

The key can be in a relational technique called "differentiation." Differentiation means drawing a clear line between yourself and your spouse, and learning to speak up for what you believe in a loving but effective way. The opposite of differentiation is emotional fusion: when you and your spouse are so entwined emotionally that when one of you is having a crisis, the other can't help but be sucked in. It's healthier for individuals to stand on their own two feet, so that one or both can remain balanced and bring needed perspective to a situation.

Here's how differentiation has worked for Kim and David:

> David's foray into day trading followed on the heels of a start-up retail business. There were many reasons why that venture didn't work out the way he wanted it to, and it was disappointing to both of us. Together, these two endeavors ate up about eighteen months of Dave's time and optimism, by the end of which we were both feeling very run down and burned out. When he decided to conclude

his day trading experiment, his natural response was to start looking for another entrepreneurial venture to get into. But I really wanted him just to work for an established company and get a regular paycheck coming in! I didn't care if he changed jobs a time or two in searching for the best opportunity, but I was positive I didn't want to watch him start yet another new business.

On a Saturday morning, I sat down with David and spoke up about what I felt I needed in terms of his career direction at this juncture. I said, "Honey, I'm sorry it hasn't worked out for you to build your own company right now. I know that's what you really desire. But I need you to know what effect your path has had on me these past eighteen months. I am tired of the constant challenges and changes. I don't feel that I can handle watching any more business ventures on your part. What I really need is a break from the craziness and uncertainty, and so do you. I'm asking you for a two-year ban on all new business start-up ventures so that we can get back on our feet financially and emotionally. I need for you to get a regular job and stick with it at least two years. I'm not saying I never want you to go into business for yourself again, but for right now I need two years away from that scene."

I didn't get hysterical as I was saying this; I didn't cry; I didn't say, "I told you so." I kept under control and made my stand. If I had gotten upset and cried, or made angry accusations, or gotten irrational—I would have been operating in emotional fusion, not differentiation.

David was rather surprised by my bold stand, but he respected me for it and really, perhaps for the first time, understood where I was coming from. Fortunately he accepted my request and agreed to the two-year moratorium. David found a job with an established company in the field of advertising where he had experienced success before his entrepreneurial ventures. This new company allows him a great deal of autonomy, and he even gets to work from his home office. So David practically feels self-employed, although he is technically an employee with a biweekly paycheck and benefits. God has given him the best of both worlds and he's never been happier!

Assuming Steve and Christine can discuss their situation as Kim and David did (it may need to be done with a counselor) and reach an agreement, Chuck recommends that Steve get an accountability partner. The concept of an accountability partner is widely used in the secular world but frequently is missing in the Christian community. Steve should have another male—his pastor, Bible study leader, a counselor, or a solid Christian friend—who will meet with him periodically to hold him to the promise he has made to Christine. This takes Christine out of the dangerous position of being the bad cop. It also gives Steve someone he respects on whom he can vent his frustrations without causing undue stress to Christine.

Christine has accepted that Steve is different. She now needs to give him some credit for his optimism and for the fact that he keeps trying and has not given up in despair. She needs to realize that Steve will probably never have the long-term security she observed in her childhood home—society is no longer structured that way and Steve was never wired that way. If Christine can make these changes in her attitudes and behaviors, and if Steve is willing to make a short-term commitment that will allow them to build up some savings, Christine will have a better sense of security and will be more accepting of Steve's future transitions. Kim says,

> I wish I had realized sooner about keeping my eyes on God for my family's security. I wish I would have known earlier about God's design for men like my husband, as well as society's influence on their behavior. But I am so thankful that these lessons have only taken the first fourteen years of our marriage! I believe we will have at least that many and more of harmony between us—no matter what direction David's career takes.

DEPRESSION

While Steve has remained optimistic overall, which is typical of his personality, Christine is concerned for the depression he faces after a failure. The Powerful Choleric is typically fairly stable emotionally, but the Popular Sanguine is known for emotional ups and downs—very up when things are going well and covered with a huge black cloud when things are not. So though Steve's depression is probably not life threatening, it is wearing on Christine and is detrimental to their marriage. It needs some attention.

Margie faced a situation similar to Christine's in her marriage. She says,

> My husband had several disappointments in the corporate world and stepped into an entrepreneurial opportunity. It failed and we lost a huge investment as well as our retirement monies. It began a downward spiral of depression.

When Margie's husband was able to find another job, it required that he be away from home and the family during the week. This plus the effects of his depression and recession from reality "cannot be repaired," Margie reports.

> While I could see the obvious signs of depression years ago, I could not get him to acknowledge it, let alone do anything about it. He simply moved farther away, both in his work and emotions. Unfortunately I did not understand the repercussions. Had I sought help, I believe we would have saved everyone in our family

tremendous problems, pain, grief, and even perhaps the impending divorce. The problem just kept building until the dam burst!

With this background, Margie encourages Christine and Steve to get professional counseling to look at the reasons for his frequent job changes: "Demand it if necessary. He is at risk and so is your future security."

Georgia Shaffer, Pennsylvania-licensed psychologist, agrees with Margie. She sees that Steve sounds unsure of himself. Georgia suggests counseling for Steve to address career and confidence.

As Christine is able to adjust her attitudes and behaviors, she will be able to be more supportive of Steve. Her acceptance is apt to remove some of the pressure from him, thereby lessening his potential for depression when things do not work out. When Christine's security comes from Christ, she will have peace. While she hopes Steve's efforts will pay off and that he does find the right position for his skills and personality, she can love and respect him for his many other qualities—the ones that attracted her to him in the first place. Kim and David worked to focus on those good qualities in their relationship. She told me,

> Even throughout the toughest times in David's career, we have worked to find areas of mutual enjoyment in our lives. We love to travel together. Sometimes we could afford only a brief weekend getaway, but we've treasured those times. We also love to take walks on the beach. It's good for our bodies and souls. We like eating out and going to movies, when finances allow. We both love trivia, so we'll quiz each other out of books or articles we've read. The point is not to lose sight of what is good and positive in your marriage, no matter what the challenges are.

After all, this is what the modern marriage is about. It is different from what many of us saw in our parents' marriage—yet the core needs of love, trust, and respect remain. Trust and respect are not based on a paycheck, dollars, or business. While society places a high value on these monetary indicators, real love, a real relationship, rises above that—that is love extravagant!

Interaction

1. The couple is to agree upon a Christian friend to whom the husband will be accountable. He will not make any job changes without the go-ahead of the accountability partner. This frees the wife from having to be the cop, restraining him from job or entrepreneurial changes.

2. The wife must make a commitment to be an emotional support and

encouragement to the husband. Building his self-esteem may contribute to his job success. She might bring him lunch, send him cards or flowers, or celebrate with his favorite meal when he meets certain milestones—these might be major sales or so many months on the job.

3. The couple is to discuss, agree upon, and write out short- and long-term joint goals. The husband's job/career plans can then be measured against the goals.

4. Diagram a career map. This map might be words and/or pictures or even cartoons—the first things that come to mind—that illustrate his various jobs and the elements that he especially liked and/or disliked. Additionally, add how he felt during that job. The jobs may indicate an up-and-down pattern to his moods. This is important, as fun is a vital aspect for his personality type. Next, search for the commonalities within the strengths and weaknesses of each position. This will help him learn what to avoid for the future and, more importantly, what he is looking for in a job—fun, respect, reward, and so on.

Twenty-Four / Seven
Togetherness

Separate Business and Personal Life

The Issue

Wes and Tina own a retail business and have worked together for the past thirteen years. During this time they have encountered a variety of challenges and, because their Personalities are very different, usually approach them differently. The fact that Tina is a Christian and Wes is not affects how they view the importance of the business in their life and how it affects their lives overall. As a man, Wes' sense of identity and worth revolves around the success or failure of the business much more than Tina's does.

Through many discussions and arguments over the years, they have learned how to work pretty well together. Wes and Tina recognize their different strengths and weaknesses that bring balance to the relationship. They have also realized that there can be only one "boss" with ultimate responsibility for decision-making. Decisions are discussed regarding policies or employees, for example, but Wes has the final say. Basically they get along great, love each other, usually like each other, and have a wonderful time when they are away from their normal routine. They enjoy the business most of the time.

Their biggest challenge has been—and continues to be—how to separate their business life from their personal life. They live in a small town and see the people who shop in their store everywhere they go. They are together every day, and everything that happens at work goes home with them and affects the mood there. Wes and Tina have no children on whom to focus their attention; there is nothing new to share about the day because each already knows exactly what went on.

If they have a disagreement about how to handle a problem at work, they can't help but take it personally, even though they know they shouldn't. Then it affects their relationship as husband and wife.

Insights

Many couples need to work at spending time together. For those in business together, one of the challenges is spending time apart! The business can easily become all-consuming. The same can be true for couples who are together in ministry. Bob and Sherrie share the same frustrations that Wes and Tina described. Sherrie says,

> My husband, Bob, and his six brothers and one brother-in-law have an incorporated farming business located in three states. We live at work; our lives revolve around the farm. When we gather at family social events, the discussion is farming. At times the wives have threatened mutiny, but being God-fearing, submissive, committed wives we've tried other means to obtain some marital and family separateness. We—the other wives and I—felt like our entire lives were one huge Jell-O mold. Our social life, our children, our church life, our financial concerns, and we were all chopped up and mixed into the farm Jell-O. Believe me, more than one of us was on antidepressants before our husbands collectively addressed the issue.

Wes and Tina have a retail business. Bob and Sherrie have a farm. While some of the tasks may be very different, many of the same problems arise—as you will see from the comments shared here. For most couples who work together, the issues seem to boil down to two specific areas: business and personal.

BETTER BUSINESS

Wes and Tina's story indicates that through "disagreements and arguments" they have already discovered a problem area common to many couples in business together: different strengths and weaknesses.

Whenever I speak on marriage and how Chuck and I are opposites, heads nod in agreement to the idea that we usually marry someone whose Personality is opposite from our own.[1] Because this is often a source of conflict, people question God's wisdom in this natural attraction. I believe that when God said the two will become one (Genesis 2:24) he had the opposite Personalities in mind. Because Chuck and I have very different strengths and weaknesses, we balance out and stabilize each other. Where I am weak, he is strong, and where he is less gifted, I am more skilled. Together we bring a full complement of talents to the table. When we can understand this we can use it to our advantage.

When a husband and wife run a business together, these differences can be a terrific asset or they can be a terrible detriment. It's great that between the two, virtually all skills needed to run the business can be found. Once they understood their personalities, Bob and Sherrie found they worked together much better in their family farm business:

> We pay a lot of attention to our Personality traits. This helps immensely! Understanding why the other ticked the way they did allowed us to delegate certain aspects of our life apart from the farm. For instance, Bob took on the budget and set up a system that keeps us on the same page without cumbersome and repeated arguments. I was responsible to keep a "honey-do" list running so that in his spare time he could get to the home repairs. He keeps the vehicles fueled and serviced; I keep up the laundry.

The difficulties arise when both spouses have a large percentage of Powerful Choleric or when the Personality type runs contrary to expected gender-specific roles. When husband and wife have the Powerful Choleric Personality in common—which is often the case when a couple is in business together—they tend to battle for control. This was the case for Tony and Amanda. They owned a photo lab for several years. The front of the shop was a retail store, where they sold cameras and related items and took in film for processing. The back contained the lab and all the equipment to process the film. Amanda reports,

> We basically split the business in two parts. Tony functioned as the technician, in charge of everything in the lab, and I was the up-front person, in charge of everything in the store. This fit our Personalities perfectly. I am Popular Sanguine and Powerful Choleric, and he is Perfect Melancholy and Powerful Choleric. He was the boss behind the door and I was the boss in front of the door. Although we made decisions together, we still had our own domains to manage. This kept us from running over each other, both mentally and physically! It worked very well and we never had problems of power—amazing for two people heavy with Powerful Choleric Personality!

Chuck and I have this same personality blend in our marriage. We are not in business together day in and day out, but we have been working on this book together. While both of us are naturally "take charge" people, we have had to divide up duties. We agreed before we ever started who would do what, and we have honored our plans. Since I am the writer and he is the therapist, we agreed that I would be the one to actually write the book. His fingers have never touched the keyboard. We have reviewed the scenarios, discussed ideas, and worked on it together. I have worked on the areas of my strengths and he on his.

If one spouse is more naturally gifted in a specific area, it would be foolish to give the other authority over that domain. My parents have been in ministry together for years and share this same Personality combination. They, too, have divided the duties. My mother as the gifted professional speaker is in charge of the stage, the "up front," and my father with a background in business is in charge of everything behind the scenes. Occasionally they share the platform, but since that is my mother's expertise, she is in charge of what goes on there. While they may discuss business or financial dealings, that is my father's turf.

This division of labor works well when two Powerful Cholerics are involved in business together—whether or not they are married. But it is essential when you are married to your business partner. You can't fire him or her, and you have to go home and sleep together. As Wes and Tina's scenario points out, while you try not to take it personally, you do take the disagreements home with you. So it is best to set things up in such a way that conflicts are minimized.

One way to do this is to agree on alternate days to be the decision maker at work. Chuck says,

> Accepting authority and exerting authority are opposite sides of the same coin. One must be able to be a good private to be a good general. By agreeing to trade off who makes the decisions, you avoid a "one up, one down relationship" which is counter to the scriptural concept of mutual submission.

There are times when stalemates will happen, no matter what. Kurt and Stephanie share some of the same concerns expressed by Wes and Tina. They each have their own business, and both businesses are run out of their home. Stephanie says,

> When we can't arrive at a mutually agreeable solution or arrive at a compromise, we often wait and don't make a decision at all. This allows us both time to reevaluate the situation. Many times things do not need to be decided right away. I believe that God has given us a hierarchy to follow, and Kurt and I have established that his decisions are the final ones. This only works if the other spouse lives by

these terms and does not pout or try to sway the other into changing his or her mind. Two bosses never works.

While some women may have trouble with Stephanie's approach, someone has to have 51 percent of the vote. Scripturally that is to be the man. 1 Corinthians 11:3 (NLT) says,

> But there is one thing I want you to know: A man is responsible to Christ, a woman is responsible to her husband, and Christ is responsible to God.

Addressing that verse, the *Life Application Bible* study notes say,

> Submission is a key element in the smooth functioning of any business, government, or family. God ordained submission in certain relationships to prevent chaos. It is essential to understand that submission is not surrender, withdrawal, or apathy. It does not mean inferiority, because God created all people in his image and because all have equal value. Submission is mutual commitment and cooperation.[2]

Opposite personalities married to each other and in business together can also be a problem when the Personality types are contrary to traditional gender roles, as is the case with my sister, Lauren, and her husband, Randy. She is naturally gifted in business and has a head for numbers. Randy, a historian, is gifted in his field and highly respected for his expertise, honesty, and integrity in an industry wrought with deception. Randy began working in the stamp and coin store when he was only twelve years old to fund his own collections. Today he and his partner own the sixty-five-year-old business that deals with stamps, coins, precious metals, and other collectibles and antiquities.

Lauren was brought in to the business because she had skills that would be an asset to the organization and would free up Randy to do what he does best. Being a Powerful Choleric, she is a natural problem-solver. Once on site day in and day out, she began to reshape the way things were done. She brought the business from no computers—everything done by hand, "but we've always done it this way"—to computerization, Web site development, and Internet trading—but not without resistance. As the Peaceful Phlegmatic who doesn't like change, Randy did not always see the need for the advancements Lauren was pushing.

In looking back over the last twenty years in business together, Lauren sees that the key thing is to have respect for each other. As a Powerful Choleric, it could be easy for her to overlook Randy's less up-front skills. As a Peaceful Phlegmatic, Randy could easily resent her obvious skills. Over the years they have learned to work together by appreciating each other's abilities and realizing that their talents lie in very different areas—both of which are needed in the business. While Lauren holds the aptitude for the more typically male tasks, it would be foolish for Randy to do them. While he is capable of fulfilling these duties, they are not in the realm of his gifts and therefore it takes him longer to do them than it takes Lauren. Since he does not enjoy the tasks, he puts them off. Most importantly, when Lauren works where she is most effective, Randy can work where he is at his best. Together they bring a full complement of skills to the table.

However, typical male/female expectations created some initial stress for them. It appeared that Lauren was trying to take over. From her viewpoint, she was just fixing the problems and making things better. They had to discuss which areas were Lauren's and which were Randy's.

Additionally, they had to learn in what areas Randy wanted Lauren's input and where he did not. Part of Randy's inherent personality is an eye for the negative. He would be thinking out loud about a problem that had been a part of the business for years. Hearing him talk about an issue, Lauren's natural problem-solving ability kicked in. She began to offer solutions. He resisted her advice, and she was frustrated when her suggestions were not implemented and the same issues were brought up again at a later date. They have worked to define what they do or do not want. When Randy complains, Lauren now asks, "Do you want a solution for this?" Or Randy may say at the beginning of a conversation, "I just want to air my thoughts. I am not looking for a solution." Lauren then knows to take off her business partner hat and put on her caring-wife demeanor. Just this has made a big difference in their working relationship.

Blaine and Golden have similar circumstances, but their working together is in ministry. Blaine reports,

Golden and I have worked together both in ministry and in the business world. Our first venture together was in ministry, and we thought it would be wonderful. But the excitement and anticipation of this new calling quickly evaporated. What were once our two individual worlds, eight-to-five, five days a week, was now one world, twenty-four/seven. It was not wonderful. In fact, it was so bad that it led us to the precipice of near divorce. Slowly we began to gravitate to the areas in which each excelled. As a Peaceful Phlegmatic with some Popular Sanguine tendencies, I have good people skills, reasonably good vision for a task, and a good work ethic. Golden, with her Powerful Choleric and Perfect Melancholy Personality, is organized, insightful, and creative.

In the business world, we ran a tourist lodge in a ski town for six years. I ran the front desk, managed the housekeeping staff, and took care of maintenance.

Golden took care of payroll, ordered supplies, and kept the books. This worked for us, as we had matured to the point that we appreciated each other's strengths and weaknesses and functioned well in our respective areas.

Understanding each other's personality—strengths and weaknesses—and defining who is in charge of what, regardless of gender, are two things that can make business better for couples who work together. One problem that seems to be shared by all couples in business together is maintaining a personal life apart from the business.

PERSONAL LIFE

Everyone who responded to Wes and Tina's situation agreed that separating business life from personal life is one of the biggest challenges. Maxine and her husband operated their own accounting firm for nearly nineteen years. She speaks for many couples that work together when she says,

> Although there are many benefits to working together, it is probably one of the most difficult relationships to find balance in as a couple.

To find that balance, Chuck suggests that Wes and Tina develop some sort of a ritual or buffer between work and homelife that will allow them to take off the "work" hat and shed the "work" clothing.

> Go to a gym, go jogging, walk the dog, do some relaxation exercises, study the Bible—anything that will pair a physical action with the cognitive process of mentally changing hats. The goal is to stop thinking about work and start thinking about the home life. We are all made up of different "selves" or "personas." There may be a professional self, a personal self, a husband or wife, a parent, and so on. Much of the difficulty people experience in communication is rooted in confusing our roles and the parameters that go with them. When the military officer comes home and lines the family up for inspection, trouble follows. A change of thinking is needed. However, it is hard to stop a thought process or drop a persona that has been used successfully all day. It is easier to change what we're doing, to change our behavior. This is why creating an actual buffer between home and work is important.

Next, he advises that they create a work-free time or "zone." They might agree that from 6:30 P.M. to 7:00 A.M. is personal time and that work will not be discussed in any way during those hours. The work-free zone might mean that you agree not to discuss work at the dinner table or in the bedroom. Chuck says,

Do the best you can. Turn off the cell phone and forward the home phone to voice mail or just let it ring. . . . Wes and Tina could institute a "work-free game." Each time someone talks about work during the agreed upon work-free time, they would chip twenty-five cents into a date fund.

These ideas will help them have a separation between the home and business worlds. Additionally, they need to develop balance in their lives, both individually and together. Addressing that need for balance, Michelle Holman, MA, LPC, observed that Wes and Tina do not seem to have anything going on in their life that does not revolve around work. She offers Tina the following advice.

I would encourage her to utilize a small group of church friends to give her an alternate place to vent and have fun. Our world can grow so large that it strains the relationships in the home, but its growing too small will have the same effect. Having a "lunch buddy" whom she meets with weekly, someone separate from her work and married life, might be another way to develop additional quality relationships.

Amanda agrees. Remembering when she and her husband were in business together she says,

I longed for girl friends and sometimes felt trapped. Sometimes all our time together was very difficult. We were together twenty-four/seven and that's too close for comfort. There was not enough space to be our own selves.

Carey and his wife are also in business together. He says,

We, too, live in a small town. We are very visible, so we feel like we are never away from our jobs. A couple of things that have helped us might be beneficial to Wes and Tina as well. First, we spend as much time apart as we can—pursuing separate interests—so that we have something to talk about. I try to have "guy nights" where I have some friends over and we watch sci-fi movies and eat pizza. My wife takes our son to a friend's house or goes to a scrapbooking party or goes shopping with a friend.

Chuck applauds the efforts that Carey and his wife have made to develop individual interests. He says,

Couples that work and live together can have a little too much togetherness. They can become emotionally enmeshed. Somewhere between detached and enmeshed is a healthy balance that will be different for each couple. Healthy couples have intimacy, yet make allowances for distance.

So Wes and Tina are encouraged to develop individual interests and friendships to give them some time apart, to help them grow and develop conversation that does not revolve around the business. Cokie and Steven Roberts advise,

> The notion that you have to choose between personal growth and marital harmony is profoundly wrong. A good marriage makes growth more possible, not less, because you have the advice and encouragement of someone who loves you.[3]

In addition to the individual things they can do, Wes and Tina also need to put some effort and creativity into doing things together that are totally different from their daily lives. Chapter 2, "Lack of Time Together," offers several suggestions for creative time together that may be helpful to Wes and Tina and all couples in business together. Couples agree that creativity is one key that has helped keep their relationship fresh and interesting.

Carey continues,

> We try to schedule one date night a month where we get out of our small town and do something out of the ordinary. It doesn't have to be expensive, but it does have to be creative. We have gone to a museum on a Friday night where they have chamber music and appetizers that you can enjoy for just the admission price. We have also gone inline skating and attended softball games and pigged out on junk food and we've tried new restaurants in our area. Every six months or so we try to arrange for childcare and get out of town for a romantic weekend. It takes creativity and work, but you can have separate hobbies and find things to talk about, even when you work together.

Bob and Sherrie found that date nights worked well for them too. However, they had to set some ground rules. Sherrie says,

> Bob and I scheduled "date nights," which we kept whether or not we wanted to. The only criterion was that we *not* discuss the farm in any way! At first it was awkward; we found we had little to talk about. We got one of those marriage builder books that sets up discussion topics. Again it was awkward and felt mechanical, but we needed a jump-start. As time went on, we would jot down things we wanted to share with one another on our date.

Maxine and her husband found that they too needed to get out of their comfort zone and do something totally different. She says,

> A balance needed to be found that would keep business at the office and our personal lives flourishing after five o'clock. Since our social life as a couple really

needed a boost, it was a godsend when we were invited to join a square dance club. This would definitely take us out of our normal element and away from the financial lingo that dominated our lives day-in and day-out. Both of us liked dancing so we said yes. This simple activity soon relieved the tension between us. Fun was returning to our relationship as we touched with a do-si-do attitude. You can't dance together without "yellow-rocking" (hugging) and letting the beat move you in a new mental direction. Laughter came back as this energetic social setting carried us one tip at a time, one festival at a time through the years. Each of us began to pursue individual interests as well. My husband joined a bowling league and I a writers group. Now we both have lots of new conversation to enrich our lives together.

Bottom line: make time for yourself; make time to keep fun in the marriage. It pays big dividends.

For Wes and Tina, for all couples in business together, loving each other with extravagance may mean adjusting their expectations of their professional selves based on personality rather than gender roles. It may mean being willing to divide responsibilities or trade off days of being the "boss." As Maxine said, make time for yourself and make time to keep fun in the marriage. In all cases, the business is secondary to the marriage; it must be your priority. Follow the suggestions found here, love extravagantly, and you'll find "it pays big dividends!"

Interaction

1. Develop a buffer between work and home. The husband and wife should each design and implement a daily after-work "buffer." This may be as simple as leaving a hat in the car or the gold jacket in the office—if that works. Most people need a more complex ritual. Physical activity with repetitive motion, such as watching one foot go in front of the other while running or watching the front wheel go around on a bicycle, is good. Change into your exercise clothes on your way out of work. Think about your breath going in and out and pair this with self-talk, saying, "I am not at work anymore. I will not think about work again until the alarm goes off tomorrow." Develop a plan for walking in the front door of your home: "First thing I am going to do is hug my wife, then I am going to hug the kids." Be creative. Do what you have to do.

2. Create a work-free time or zone. Schedule and implement a time or place when work will not be discussed in any way. This could be from 6:30–8:30 each evening or while in the dining room or bedroom. Bring your home under your control. It may also be necessary to designate a scheduled time to "vent" about

work. Learn how to commiserate and say, "Poor baby." Avoid projecting anger about someone else onto your spouse. Your spouse is the last person you want to get mad at. Get the frustration out so you can focus on the here and now.

3. Design a "work-free zone" game. Create and implement a fun game that tracks the violations of the "work-free zone." Write out the rules on a poster. This will help make the unconscious tendency to lapse back into the work role conscious and under your control. The couple might decide to put twenty-five cents into a piggy bank for each violation. There could be a whistle blown to signal a foul. The offender might agree to give the other spouse a five-minute back rub. Be creative. The crazy stuff will stay in your memory.

4. Develop something all your own. Each spouse should identify and develop an activity that is solely his or her own. Time should be set aside, guilt-free, to invest in this aspect of yourself. It is also important to budget money for these activities. Additionally, each spouse should select a personal space in the home that is just his or hers. This could be a corner for a piano or a sewing machine, or room in the garage for a roll-about toolbox. Trust and respect in a marriage require the opportunity for privacy and security. This is especially important for Perfect Melancholies.

2

FINANCIAL
ISSUES

Chapter
SEVEN

Orchestrate Finances

Prenuptial Agreements, Trust, Connecting

The Issue

Kathy and Mark are newly married. She is thirty-nine and he is forty-four. It is a second marriage for both of them. They are both strong financially. Mark has built a successful business and Kathy is part owner of her father's real estate business and holdings—which has supported her and her daughter for the last fifteen years. However, Kathy is finding it difficult to orchestrate finances with Mark. In an attempt to honor her father and help him not to feel threatened, Mark and Kathy agreed to sign a prenuptial agreement, keeping their finances separate. Now Mark is feeling threatened by the influence of his father-in-law.

They contribute equally to a joint account that pays their household expenses, but they are finding it difficult to feel connected in their marriage. There is no real sense of working together for their future or for that of their four children (three are his and one is hers). Mark struggles with the fact that he is not truly the provider for the family. They are trying to find a middle ground to avoid having to separate totally from her father's business in order to have peace. The agreement seemed like a good idea and smart in a business sense in the beginning, but now it makes their marriage feel like a business arrangement instead of a "one flesh" union.

Insights

This particular dilemma presents two specific issues common to many modern marriages. One is the merging of two financial houses and styles of money management—often based in a prenuptial agreement—and the other is developing a sense of connectedness in the new family. As you will see, other couples in similar circumstances, as well as the contributing therapists, recognize these as two different, possibly unrelated, situations.

PRENUPTIAL AGREEMENTS

In an Ozzie-and-Harriet world, prenuptial agreements were not an issue. Couples usually married young before either had an opportunity to acquire anything. They started out in a small apartment with nothing but their wedding presents and some borrowed furniture. Together they built what became their net worth. She raised the children and managed the home responsibly while offering him the emotional support he needed to function at his best as he earned the family income. There was no need for a prenuptial agreement. Chuck's grandparents, "Ma and Pa," were married seventy-five years. Over the years, Pa told his grandchildren the story of their wedding day. As they left the marriage ceremony Pa realized that he had one coin in his pocket. He took it out and tossed it over his left shoulder so he and Ma could start out "even."

Today many marriages face similar situations to that of Kathy and Mark. When one or both spouses is established financially, has their own investments, and is used to being in control of their own monetary destiny, it is very difficult to let go completely and offer the spouse everything one has worked so hard to achieve. This is especially true when either or both the husband and wife have a history with a former spouse where money was either spent foolishly or used as a tool for control.

Sherrie's history with her former husband colored her new marriage:

> From experience, I can say that second marriages are prone to over-sensitivity. The couple doesn't start from ground zero when it comes to building a life together. We often enter the marriage with wounds and sensitivities—some have been healed, others remain hidden. Though our financial situation was composed of different elements than Kathy and Mark's, my husband and I were both uptight in the money arena. I chose to give up my career in the city to become a farmer's wife and a stay-at-home mom. In addition to feeling like a "slacker" for not contributing to the household budget, I felt powerless and vulnerable. I worried about being abandoned again.

The world's resolution for this modern marriage problem is the prenuptial agreement. However, there is no scriptural foundation for this concept, and it is adverse to the biblical concept of "leave and cleave."

Chuck has found that whatever the situation, a prenuptial agreement is "pure

poison." He would never suggest a prenuptial agreement in premarital counseling.
Gaylen Larson, Ph.D., agrees:

> The problem with a prenuptial agreement is that it says, "I don't trust you or this
> relationship to last." As trust is a core basis of any marriage, a prenuptial agree-
> ment is just the opposite of what is needed.

But since Kathy and Mark already have one, Chuck would suggest that Kathy
and Mark develop a plan to begin to phase out the agreement. They need to think
about how long they would have to be married to be able to trust each other. For
example, he asks, "If you are married twenty years, would you still need a prenuptial agreement?" Most couples he has counseled scoff at the thought of needing
such an agreement after twenty years. "What about ten? What about five?" he asks.
Together they need to discuss at what point the prenuptial agreement would be a
moot issue and plan to phase it out accordingly.

Maxine Marsolini, author of *Blended Families*, adds,

> Trust between the two of them needs to form throughout the marriage and the
> stepfamily before the agreement should be done away with entirely. After reading
> the issues between Mark and Kathy, I sense them blaming the prenuptial agree-
> ment for their inability to set goals for their blended family. Realize it is always
> possible to set family financial goals. There is money going into the joint account.
> The question is, are you willing to work together in the best interest of every
> family member? Too many women get taken in by a charming man only to find
> that a couple of years later he has gone through all their holdings and they are left
> with meager funds. Until trust is built, and Mark's self-image is not threatened by
> this premarital agreement, it is reasonable for Kathy to retain the written contract.
> After all, she also has a responsibility to the business partnership she holds with
> her father.

Reanna found that trust was a key issue in her marriage to Tim. Both had been
married before. When they had a prenuptial agreement drawn up, Reanna had
convinced herself that it was really to protect Tim from her student loan problems
with the potential threat of having her bank account attached. But, she says,

> As time has gone by, I have realized that [the prenuptial agreement] is really about
> my wanting to retain my independence, not trusting Tim with finances, and not
> wanting to answer to anyone about how I spent my money.

Now that Reanna and Tim have been married for seven years, Reanna can see the error of her ways and they are taking steps to correct their situation. She continues,

> Tim has never wanted to do things this way. I always felt like I needed to control "my money." Since I bring in more than he does, I have felt that I have a right. Now I can see that we do not have a complete union. We split up bills like roommates. God has been speaking to my heart about our separateness in financial affairs. It has been the source of nearly all our arguments. I have been in bondage to money as a result. I have lifted this up in prayer—wanting to stop depending on myself for financial security. I know that I need to trust my husband with the finances, and by putting things into God's order of things, I am relieved of the burden. This has been a process where God has been changing my heart. This is not something that can be worked out logically as much as spiritually. I could have handed these things over to Tim from the beginning, but then I would have been resentful and still trying to control things. God has been doing a work in me from the inside out.

Reanna encourages Kathy and Mark to do some soul searching and come to a place of trust.

Reanna is right: "This is not something that can be worked out logically." If we go with logic alone, a prenuptial agreement might sound like a good idea. I remember my attorney's advice before I got married. Since I owned my own business and some real estate, he suggested that Chuck and I have a prenuptial agreement. When I listened to his side, it sounded logical. I approached Chuck about it. Chuck's reaction was much like that of Pat and Vito. Pat shared,

> My husband and I are both in a second marriage and my son (who is the only child) wanted me to have a prenuptial agreement drawn up. After talking with my attorney about it, it seemed the main purpose a prenuptial agreement serves is in the event of a divorce. Since we were making this commitment for the rest of our lives, it really did not seem relevant to even remotely plan for a divorce to happen.

Chuck felt that creating a prenuptial agreement was like planning to fail and I agreed. We did not draw one up either.

While a prenuptial agreement makes sense in the ways of the world, it gets down to the question, what are you really committed to? The money or the marriage? Part of being married is dying to self—loving extravagantly.

Stephanie and Kurt also had a prenuptial agreement when they got married. Stephanie reports,

It was a second marriage for both of us. It wasn't until we started attending some marriage classes that we realized this agreement was totally against God's plan for marriages. True "one-flesh" marriage includes the income. Kurt and I each own our own businesses. We don't always agree on policies and procedures, but we are in agreement that all our income is ours—not his or mine. We have learned to totally depend on the Lord for our finances. After all, all of our blessings, income, and material gain are His and come from Him. We would urge all couples to do as we did. We burned our agreement at a group meeting—made it public. It was a real testimony. Christians need to learn to stand up for what God has instituted and not compromise.

If you have a prenuptial agreement, whether official and legal or simply verbally agreed on, look at the cause of its existence. Are there trust and/or control issues present? Is your relationship now at a place where you can begin to phase it out or tear it up as Stephanie and Kurt did? Whichever direction you determine is right for the equilibrium of your situation, if you have a prenuptial agreement in place, get some specific guidance before abandoning it so you do not create legal trouble for yourself. Chuck advises that if an agreement puts one spouse in a position above the other—a "one up/one down," it can only do damage to the marriage. In cases where some financial protection is needed, there are other ways to work it out that do not pit one spouse against the other. When Pat and Vito got married, they set up a trust fund for her son instead of a prenuptial agreement. It has worked out well for all involved.

Beyond the basic problems many couples face with a prenuptial agreement, Kathy's situation is muddied even further by the fact that her finances are intermingled with her father's. Rose Sweet, pastoral counselor and author, advises Kathy from her own experience:

Kathy needs to leave her father and mother as Scripture says (Genesis 2:24) and trust God to take care of her through her husband. For twenty-one years I have worked for and with my father in the company he started and have been the "owner" of the family business—during which time I was both married and divorced. I know both sides. I can understand Kathy's fears. The bottom line is that Kathy has put her financial security and her father's emotional concerns above her marriage. Honoring her father does not mean meeting his emotional needs; rather she should take them into consideration before she and her husband make their final decisions.

While Chuck and I did not have a prenuptial agreement, we did face some of the same problems Kathy and Mark are facing. I owned my own business when we got married. Trends changed, and about seven years into our marriage I had to close my business and find another source of income. For several years I struggled to earn a living from a variety of sources. What seemed to be the best fit evolved from the work I had been doing with my parents. Eventually I joined them in their business and became a vital part of their activities—earning more than I had ever made before or since. This was my best period of income, but it was the worst time for my marriage.

I was constantly torn between my parents and honoring them and cleaving to my husband. We reached a crisis point where I had to be willing to walk away from the security the family business provided and place my husband and my marriage first. The end result was that I did not have to find an entirely new career or leave the family business, but I had to be willing to do so. Eventually we found a plan that worked for everyone involved. I now own a portion of what was once my parents' business, which I run as I see fit without their involvement. My parents still own the part of the business that was their passion from the start. We operate cooperatively but independently. From my experience, I would encourage Kathy to look at ways they might be able to restructure her professional relationship with her father before a crisis in her marriage develops.

From his experience as a therapist, Chuck discourages adults working for their parents. It can be successful, but working for one's parents makes the process of reaching peerhood with your parents very difficult. Failing to reach peerhood with parents can result in husband and wife being on unequal footing—with one "parenting" the other.

CREATING CONNECTEDNESS

Kathy and Mark also have a need for a sense of working together in their marriage. This is not strictly a financial issue but more one of personal development. Many couples face this problem even when there are no monetary issues. Michelle Holman, MA, LPC, would work with Kathy and Mark to help them understand that intimacy involves more than sharing business goals. She says,

> Intimacy comes from being an authentic individual who shares with someone else one's true self and is willing to risk the vulnerability that comes with this. If Kathy and Mark are simply wanting to be more connected in their finances, the joint household account's purposes could be enlarged to include contributing to family goals such as children's education, vacations, and special activities.

Kathy states that Mark does not feel as if he is truly the provider for the family. Again, money is not the only way to provide for one's family. Mark could focus on providing spiritual leadership, being a good example for their children, and offering a shoulder to cry on when needed. All of these are much needed aspects of providing for his family. Michelle Holman says,

> If Mark is struggling with the idea that he is not truly being the provider for the family, where did he learn that he "should" be? Has he been taught tradition or Scripture? Biblically, being the head of a home doesn't mean that he must be the sole source of income. The Proverbs 31 woman contributed to her household.

Additionally, Kathy should be grateful that her husband wants to be the provider in an age when many men shirk their responsibilities.

To bring the financial and connectedness concerns together, Kathy and Mark need to work cooperatively on some joint goals. This can be done even if their prenuptial agreement remains in place or while they are working to phase it out. Jane's situation is similar, although she does not think that she and her husband ever felt less "one flesh." Their marriage is the second for both. They maintain separate accounts and have a joint account for household expenses. Jane has no children and her husband has one son. From her experience, Jane would advise Kathy and Mark:

> They should sit down together and talk about their plans for the future. If necessary, they could do this with a counselor, but they may be able to do it themselves. Establish goals as a couple. It might be helpful for each of them to make a wish list and then bring the lists together. These goals need not be financial only, but could include things like weekly Bible study together, one spouse cleaning the bathroom weekly, or a regular date night. Many couples need to work on their homes and yards. New vehicles, vacations, and retirement must be planned for. Charitable giving should also be discussed. Once they have made their lists, they need to prioritize, deciding what to tackle first and developing a time line. In this way, they will feel that they are working together to build a home and a marriage.

Working together to build a home and a marriage is what Marge and Jesse found they needed to do. Their situation was similar to Kathy and Mark's. Marge made quite a bit more money than Jesse and was reluctant to give him access to all her earnings and holdings. Her first marriage had been a financial fiasco and she was still recovering from the damage her ex-husband had caused. One of the many things they did was to take a large portion of their individual earnings and use it for joint investments. They also decided to sell the house where they were living. It had been Jesse's home before they got married and remained in his name only. They bought a new house to start together and it carries both their names on the mortgage.

Along the same lines, Melanie Wilson, Ph.D., suggests that they get involved in a financial project that involves them both. She says,

> Perhaps it is something their children could even help with. For example, the family could decide that they have a goal of buying a vacation home. They could research together where to purchase it, how much it would cost, etc. Then they could budget and invest money toward that goal. Perhaps they could research stocks or mutual funds that would help them reach the goal.

With these cooperative goals, several suggested that Kathy's income contribute more heavily toward vacations, retirement, and college funds while Mark's money could go into providing household finances. Robin Jackson, a financial software developer, suggested this solution:

> Create a college savings plan for each of the four children. Working together doesn't have to mean only one account from which all monies are drawn. A great example of this is Fidelity Investment's Unique College Investing Plan. While only one person can be the account owner with one beneficiary (the child), both spouses can contribute to the fund and watch it grow as a family. Letting the children know about their investment account and going online to check its growth can be a very good way to teach them about planning ahead, delaying gratification, and feeling secure.

Robin also suggested another option: a revocable living trust that would make a "we" out of the "he" and "she." The trust would be a legal entity that would hold the assets they want to share. She encouraged Kathy and Mark to hire a financial planner. Melanie Wilson also recommends that they involve a third party in their finances, and Chuck agrees. Having a third party involved, a financial professional, removes either spouse from the control or "cop" position and provides for more cooperative decision-making while removing the ability to blame each other for financial mistakes they may make in the future.

Chapters 9, "Paycheck to Paycheck," and 11, "Can't See the Trees for the Forest," are related and may be of help as well.

Different couples have found solutions that work for their situations. That is what the concept of equilibrium is all about. Whatever direction Kathy and Mark, or you, decide to go, pray and ask for guidance. Prayer is no place for nonsense. It is a holy place, where the innermost being of a person is revealed, where two people can share their minds and souls and find a life together.

Interaction

1. Each spouse should describe in detail the signs, behaviors, actions, and milestones that would indicate that your husband/wife could be fully trusted.

2. Each spouse should describe in detail the signs, or "fruit," that indicate a changed heart and a full commitment to you and the marriage.

3. Together set common goals for the marriage and family. Design signposts that mark progress, indicating how you will know when things are getting better.

4. Together design a phase-out schedule for the prenuptial agreement. This could be a timeline in cartoon format with signposts drawn on banner paper. (You can also include project steps one through three on the timeline.)

5. Each spouse should independently explore and describe fears surrounding giving up autonomy and control. Then brainstorm any other blocks to progress.

Chapter EIGHT

Boys and Their Toys

Control, Shared Activities

The Issue

Bruce and Janna are in their early twenties and have been married a few years. It is a first marriage for both. Bruce is a Popular Sanguine with some of the easygoing, likeable nature of the Peaceful Phlegmatic. He is in the military. Janna is almost fifty-fifty Perfect Melancholy and Powerful Choleric. She is in retail management and is going to school. When Bruce is not off on a long trip or out to sea, his work hours are very set, as is his income. Being in retail, Janna's hours are often long and can vary greatly, especially during the holidays. Add school to her schedule and she is often away from home much of the time that Bruce is off. As she has been promoted, and promoted again, her income has taken a big leap.

Bruce is due to complete his military commitment soon. At that time they hope to move and both go to college full time. Janna is the stronger personality and the more financially responsible. Bruce is more laid back, a little less mature, and more interested in having a good time. While Janna is working or going to school, Bruce spends time with "the boys" and buys "toys" to entertain himself. Janna is frustrated with him because she is trying to put money away for their college education. He feels that since she is gone, and they *do* have the money, he has a right to spend it.

Insights

Bruce and Janna have two key problems that are presented in their situation. Janna makes more money and is the stronger personality. This combination can very easily put her into a position of feeling like the parent—which is unhealthy from either spouse's perspective. Bruce can easily feel controlled by Janna and resent her behavior, while Janna resents what she perceives as his childlike behavior. We'll call this issue "control." Additionally, their lives already seem to be going separate ways with her focusing on school and work and him spending time in fun activities with his friends. They will need to find time to spend together doing things they both enjoy.

CONTROL

Anne's stomach turned with remembrance over Bruce and Janna's situation as she said, "I can definitely identify with this." While Anne and her husband's situation is the reverse of Bruce and Janna's, they had many of the same problems. In their household, Anne is the spender and her husband is the saver, the money-conscious person in the relationship. Anne reflects,

> Since the day we were married we have always given each other an allowance. While he thought this was great, I felt like a controlled child. I often resented feeling like Daddy was giving me my weekly allowance for doing my chores.

The control issue is a main concern for Bruce and Janna, especially as Janna has the stronger personality. If she does what comes naturally to her—earning money and saving responsibly—while pushing Bruce to do the same, he is likely to feel the way Anne did: like a controlled child. Only for Bruce and Janna it tends to be magnified since the female is the more "adult." Most of us were raised expecting that the male would be responsible, while society is often more forgiving of the woman who is thought of as "flighty."

As the Popular Sanguine, Anne says,

> I live for the moment, the fun of it. My husband, being a Perfect Melancholy, couldn't conceive of just stopping at Starbucks for a cup of coffee when he could brew a whole pot of it at home for less than half the cost. I, on the other hand, love spontaneity and couldn't understand his boring control. I like to enjoy life. My husband is proud of his accomplishments and the growth of his bank account. After all, in his eyes, his worth depends on it.

Anne and her husband separated after eleven years of marriage. During their three-year separation they started seeing a marriage counselor. In counseling they learned that they each needed to give a little and trust each other more. Anne learned,

I needed to understand where he was coming from. I needed to work harder at saving some money and not just living for today. Also, I needed to help him realize his worth was not in how much he could save. He needed to realize that if he let me breathe, assist with the money decisions, and relax, I would learn to be more responsible.

If Bruce and Janna do not learn some give-and-take as Anne and her husband did, they are apt to find themselves separated as well. Georgia Shaffer, Pennsylvania-licensed psychologist, agrees. She sees that each will "need to do a little 'dying to self' to make it past the rough spots."

Anne would advise Janna from her own experience to learn to compromise:

After all, you are a team. Work together like one. Above all, ask God for guidance and help. Without Him we can do nothing.

Anne mentioned that she and her husband needed to "give a little and trust each other more." This was true for Alicia and Greg, whose situation is similar to Bruce and Janna's in that Alicia is the conservative one. Greg is the spender. Alicia explains their situation:

When Greg and I got married, I brought much more money into the marriage than he had ever thought of having. Not only that, but Greg was still paying off a significant loan to his father from the debt he incurred from his first marriage. We decided to keep everything separate—separate checking and saving accounts; we split all the bills.

Chuck and I have a similar situation in that I am more of a saver and he is more of a spender—even though I am the Popular Sanguine and he is the Perfect Melancholy. I was taught to be responsible with money from a very early age and have owned my own business most of my adult life. I have had to be responsible. Like Alicia and Greg, Chuck and I have kept our finances separate with agreed-upon shared expenses. As our financial arrangements are born out of different styles of money management rather than a trust issue, this approach has worked well for us and might be a good solution for Bruce and Janna. After agreed-upon shared living expenses are met, they could settle on an amount to be put away each month for college. That money should go into a joint savings account, or better yet, into a CD or money market account, where the funds are not easily accessible and where both signatures are needed for a withdrawal. Once these funds are put away, each could spend or save as they see fit—removing the sense of one partner parenting the other.

Maxine Marsolini, author of *Blended Families*, often encounters couples with problems similar to Bruce and Janna's. She usually advises,

> Begin by forming a budget you can live with, not one that is too rigid. If you married a man who is more fun-loving than you, you can't take that quality out of him and have a happy camper. Instead use wisdom. Build a budget [together] that allows him spending within reasonable limits and still makes room for your tendency to save for future goals. This way, you will both feel respected and loved, while keeping alive the spark that drew you to that person in the beginning.

This approach has worked for Chuck and me and it worked for Alicia and Greg. However, Alicia says,

> About two-and-a-half years into our marriage, I felt that I was to trust my husband to get to the next level. I wasn't showing him complete trust and he wasn't taking pride in the money I had.

Alicia took a leap of faith, giving Greg virtually everything. They combined their accounts and Greg now takes care of the checkbook and the bills. He is in charge of their finances, although Alicia still makes sure they record every expense that they have when they have it. Alicia describes their system:

> We each have a piece of paper and a pencil in our wallets. When the money goes out, it is recorded. At the end of each month, I itemize all the expenses and the income for each month. It then goes on a graph to show where we are. Surprisingly it has worked wonderfully. We see exactly where our money is going. For instance, Greg's incremental charges on fast food can add up to $100 a month. Once he knows that, he can decide for himself if it is really worth it. When it comes to big expenses, we pray about it together before we make a decision.

They agree it has been a good experience for both of them. Alicia has learned a lesson in trust. Greg has learned to take more responsibility for his money.

They had been married several years and reached a place where Greg had demonstrated financial responsibility with his own finances before he took over their accounts. If they had not reached this level, it would have been foolish to give Greg charge of their bookkeeping. If your marriage is similar to Bruce and Janna's, you might start with budgeted, separate accounts, and later, if you agree it is the right choice, you could try what Alicia and Greg have done. Remember that each marriage relationship is shaped differently. Each has its own equilibrium and no one answer will fit every situation.

Chuck sees that Bruce and Janna are in a cycle that they must stop before applying any of these practical ideas. Bruce resents that Janna is unavailable so he spends money to get even. As their funds are drained, Janna works harder to make more money and is gone more. Bruce's resentment grows and he spends even more. Gaylen Larson, Ph.D., sees that Bruce may be acting in a passive-aggressive way:

> Bruce's spending while Janna works may be his way of dealing with his anger over her making more money than he does. I am concerned that if Bruce doesn't deal with his anger, he will eventually drive Janna away.

Once you realize that you are in this cycle, you can brainstorm solutions to break it and then apply some practical money-management techniques.

ACTIVITIES

In reviewing Bruce and Janna's situation, both Chuck and Georgia Shaffer were concerned about the apparent lack of time they spend together doing things they both enjoy—"fun time together," as Georgia called it. She sees that Bruce and Janna are moving apart by playing or working and that each will have to give up some of what they are doing to make a real go of it as a couple. Georgia suggests that Janna may need to put off school or cut back on her hours so there is more time for them as a couple, and Bruce will need to limit his time with his buddies.

Chuck agrees that they need to spend more time in joint activities. He recommends that Bruce begin taking classes now, even if it is only one class a term and that Janna become a part of the "boys'" activities. Even if what they do together is not something she enjoys, she could participate by bringing them lunch or a favorite snack or showing an interest in what they are doing. Chuck has a buddy with whom he likes to build stuff, especially welding. Currently they are working on a carriage for a cannon barrel they bought together. While I have no interest in learning to weld, I can still be involved. I can stop by and check on their progress, I can bring them cookies while they are working, and I can ask about it when Chuck gets home.

Chuck and I have activities we do together, those we do individually, and those we share, even though we would not do them without the other person. Chuck loves to mountain bike. While I find that going up and down via the power of my legs is no fun, I did buy a mountain bike so we could ride together. If he wants to ride in the foothills, he goes while I am out of town or am busy. However, I do enjoy taking the ski chairlift to the top of the mountain and riding my bike down. I also enjoy riding on the flat trail we have near our home that runs along the Rio

Grande. So we do those together. Chuck likes to scuba dive. I prefer to lie on the beach with a good book. However, I just got certified as a scuba diver. When we vacation near the water, we can now scuba dive together. I like to sail. But unless we have good strong winds giving us forward momentum, Chuck has a tendency to get sick. (He has learned to watch what he eats and to drink plenty of water before we go sailing.) Together we usually take one sailing trip a year. We each give a little and we have a lot of fun together!

Chuck says that if the husband is placed in a position where he has to choose between his wife and his friends, she can only lose. Either he chooses his wife and harbors resentment, or worse, he chooses his friends! Always leave a way out. Therefore, Chuck would encourage Janna to be a part of Bruce's circle of friends whenever possible.

If Bruce and Janna's situation sounds like your marriage, take to heart the advice of the peers and professionals offered here. Be willing to make some changes in both your attitudes and behaviors and you are bound to see some improvement in your relationship. Some similar issues are raised in chapter 2, "Lack of Time Together," and may be of help.

Interaction

1. Restructure your finances with the involvement of a bookkeeper or financial planner. Agree upon how much each spouse needs monthly for personal expenses and for joint expenses, with the remainder going toward savings or another mutually agreed upon plan. The third party is important, as this will remove the wife from the cop or parent position.

2. Develop and agree on short- and long-term goals, including future education plans. Once goals are established, determine how much must be set aside to achieve them within the desired time frame. The bookkeeper may be needed to keep them on track.

3. In every case, when you are seeking a change in your spouse, you need to ask yourself, what is the currency that my spouse values? For example, the currency for you may be money while your spouse values peace, harmony, and fun. In light of this difference, Chuck would recommend a "behavior exchange" or barter. If your spouse will agree to certain specific changes, i.e., spending twenty dollars less a week, you will quit nagging him and engage in at least one fun activity a week. Building on the exchange, your spouse will brainstorm a list of creative ways to save money. You will make a list of ways that you can bring peace, harmony, and fun into your time together. On a daily basis you will independently record how often each idea was used, and weekly get together and review progress.

Chapter NINE

Paycheck to Paycheck

Finances, Trust and Respect, Children From a
Previous Marriage

The Issue

Joe and Cindy have been married a few years. Joe is used to people loving him and caring for him. With his Popular Sanguine/Peaceful Phlegmatic Personality he has charmed people all his life and they have covered for him. Joe left his wife, the mother of his children, in search of more fun. As a result of the divorce, Joe lost his position as a pastor and got a job in the business world.

Later, at work, he met Cindy. She is sharp, aggressive, and a leader—everything his wife was not. Joe was immediately attracted to Cindy, a strong Powerful Choleric with some Perfect Melancholy. Cindy, in her late forties, has never been married before; she has been a professional all her adult life.

Most of Joe's funds go to support his four children. As a result he lives from paycheck to paycheck. Cindy's income covers the majority of their living and leisure costs.

Joe knew better than to have left his wife and children. He is plagued with guilt. Cindy feels that his children take advantage of his guilt. When his oldest daughter called him to ask for a high school graduation party at a local restaurant—which he would pay for—he gave in although he could not afford it, and could not have afforded it even before the divorce. Such extravagances were not a part of their lifestyle on his pastor's salary. Since he has no available cash, he borrowed money from his boss to pay for the party and paid it back a little each paycheck.

He made the commitment to his daughter without discussing it with Cindy, as he knew she would say no. By having the money taken out of his paycheck, he thought Cindy would never know. Of course, eventually Cindy found out. She was furious. He went behind her back and promised to pay for the party, when he could not even contribute significantly to their joint expenses.

Two years later it was time for the next daughter to graduate. In testing her father's love, she wanted a bigger party at a nicer restaurant. Again he felt guilty and gave in. Remembering the last blow up, Joe did not tell Cindy. He knew she would be angry again. When the credit card bill came, he took money from their joint account to pay it—again without telling Cindy. Cindy found out when she attempted to take some money from the account and discovered that it had been depleted.

Cindy is at her wit's end. She has always been fiscally responsible and is used to having cash at her disposal. She is ready to send Joe back to his original family— who doesn't want him back.

Insights

The obvious issue that comes into play in this situation is finances; they are often a problem in second marriages and especially so when children from previous marriages are involved. We will look separately at the issue of trust and respect, something lacking in Joe and Cindy's marriage.

FINANCES

Diana and her husband, Mike, also had to address financial issues in relationship to their marriage and their stepchildren. She says,

> I am the mother of two adult children and stepmother to my husband's two adult children from his first marriage. In our seven years of marriage we have had to come to agreement regarding financing college educations, weddings, and other needs in our children's lives.

The key here is that Diana and Mike "had to come to an agreement." This is an area apparently lacking in Joe and Cindy's situation. To avoid future problems, they need to address what is realistic for their situation and agree to make decisions together. Diana continues,

> I married Mike and his children. His financial responsibility for his children became my financial responsibility. Mike married my children and me. My financial

responsibility for my children became Mike's. In fact, my daughter was still a minor when we married, so Mike provided shelter, food, and clothing for her because she lived with us. We assisted Mike's son with his advanced education (paid for from shared funds) as well as jointly contributing financially to my son's wedding. Mike's son is getting married next year and we will again be contributing jointly toward those expenses. Each situation is discussed individually.

One perspective is that since Cindy is more skilled financially, Joe might consider turning over all of the management of their funds to her. The problem with this option is that there is already a tendency for resentment in their marriage. If financial issues are not clearly agreed upon as Diana brought up, Joe is apt to feel dominated and controlled by Cindy, creating an imbalance of power. For this approach to work, Joe and Cindy will need to clearly agree that all financial decisions are made together.

Roseanne Elling, LPC, says,

> When there is an unbalance of power in a marriage, the relationship often resembles that of parent/child rather than husband/wife. In the case of the Powerful Choleric wife and Peaceful Phlegmatic or Popular Sanguine husband, the wife seems parental (scolding, disapproving) to the less powerful personalities and the husband seems childlike (fearful, irresponsible) to the more powerful personalities. This certainly occurs regardless of gender, but it is most frustrating to a Powerful Choleric wife who longs for a partner, not a dependant. It's difficult to achieve intimacy in a relationship with an "I'm superior/more powerful; you're inferior/less able" underlying attitude.

Stephanie says she and her husband, Kurt, had similar issues during the early years of their marriage:

> When I found out Kurt was taking out loans to pay off debts, I became a wild woman. My actions did not help him to be more open, but to hide his behavior to escape my condemnation. At the time we didn't understand how important it is in a marriage to be a team with finances, gifts, business, and family. Marriage Ministries International and Christian Financial Concepts helped us discover the connection we needed to make changes.
>
> Now, as a team, we do our own finances and will be debt-free very soon. We are not wealthy, but have learned that wild spending and debt do not a happy marriage make.

Another practical option would be for Cindy and Joe to separate their finances with an agreed-upon amount going toward joint expenses. One couple figured out their individual share of payments based on a percentage of their incomes. Using this approach, anything remaining would be available for additional expenses like the graduation parties.

This is what Chuck and I have done. In fact, to remove the control issues, we have involved a third party. We have a bookkeeper who pays all our bills from a joint checking account. She then tells us how much each of us needs to contribute to that account. I write a check from my personal account and Chuck writes a check from his. Our checks are deposited into the joint account to cover the checks written against it. Neither Chuck nor I touch the joint checkbook—though we are both signers on the account. By having the third party involved, I am not telling Chuck what to do and he is not telling me what to do. Control does not become the issue. (If hiring a bookkeeper isn't an option, a trusted friend with a sense for numbers might provide the same service.)

As long as we both contribute as agreed to the joint expenses, neither of us fusses at the other about our personal spending habits. Chuck is apt to buy classic motorcycles or car parts. I am likely to bring home a new outfit when I do not need one. As long as we both meet our agreed upon obligations, these additional expenditures are not an issue. Again, the fact that we have discussed this and agreed upon the solution is paramount to the success of our approach.

TRUST AND RESPECT

Another concern for Joe and Cindy is trust and respect. Cindy cannot currently trust Joe, as his pattern has been to do things behind her back. Gaylen Larson, Ph.D., addresses the importance of trust for Joe and Cindy.

> Joe needs to realize that he is eroding trust in the marriage by his actions, causing Cindy to think, "If I can't trust him with finances, in what other areas should I not trust him?" Eventually, she will not respect him, which is a primary need. The result could easily be another divorce.

Joe probably doesn't mean to lie, rather he is trying to avoid a consequence. As a Popular Sanguine/Peaceful Phlegmatic, Joe wants everyone to be happy with him. He gives in to his children rather than disappoint them. He doesn't tell Cindy what he has done because he hopes she will never find out, thus avoiding her wrath. Joe needs to develop some backbone. He needs to grow up and accept responsibility. By discussing expenditures with Cindy he brings the issue into the open and she will learn that she can trust him.

The author of *Blended Families*, Maxine Marsolini, says,

We must realize surprises with a negative financial impact are really untold truths. When they are discovered they speak volumes about the character of a spouse. Undisclosed truths say our self-image is too fragile to entrust to our mate. In marriage that is not a good thing.

A wife or husband who discovers hidden financial issues should begin to pray for wisdom. Praise God that the secrets have surfaced. As ugly as it may seem, the truth is about to set the two of you free. Then together commit to finding a small group financial study such as is offered through Crown Financial Ministries (www.crown.org), and submit to the godly counsel your family so badly needs. These studies not only deal with budgets, but with honesty, family respect, delayed gratification, and more.

Because of societal expectations, one of the greatest problems of marriages where the female is the Powerful Choleric and the male is the Peaceful Phlegmatic is at play here: respect vs. resentment. Because the Powerful Choleric so naturally takes charge of things—usually doing a better job than the Peaceful Phlegmatic would—it is very easy to just let the Powerful Choleric female take over. While this seems like an easy option in the short run, it creates resentment in the long term. In this case, Cindy cannot respect Joe because she sees him as weak—giving in to his children's demands and being afraid to discuss them with her first. She is already building resentment toward him because she sees that he is not an adequate provider. This is where Diana's comments about accepting his previous financial obligations as her own are so important.

If Joe is willing to mature to the point that he can address the financial concerns and come to an agreement that he can stick with, Cindy will be able to respect him more, thus lessening the resentment she feels about his contributions toward their joint expenses. For the marriage to succeed, both partners need to be able to respect each other, as Shellie reminds us:

> Stephen and I have learned that respect begins when we admit not only our own weaknesses but also the other's strengths, and decide to draw from those strengths. I am generally better at keeping track of financial things, while Stephen is better at looking at our schedule commitments. We have decided to use those strengths in each other for the betterment of our relationship. He depends on me to keep track of money, and I depend on him to help me see when I have over committed and am doing too much. What were at the beginning of our marriage areas of great frustration have become—after almost fifteen years—true strengths.

CHILDREN

This scenario also presents the possibility of the children trying to sabotage their father's new marriage. While Joe should not have divorced his first wife, he did.

He is now committed in a new relationship and it is too late to go back and undo what has been done. In his book *Sacred Marriage*, Gary Thomas says,

> If you are reading this and you've already gone through a divorce, you serve no one—least of all God—by becoming fixated on something you can't undo. That's what forgiveness and grace are for—a fresh start, a new beginning.[1]

Making his new marriage work must be a priority. Joe needs to accept God's forgiveness for his sin against his first family. Some pastoral counseling might help him with this spiritual truth that, as a former pastor, he must know. Once he does this, he needs to live as one who is forgiven and not under guilt. Then he will be able to recognize and rightly respond to the manipulative behavior of his children.

Chuck sees that Joe is in the middle between Cindy and his children. Chuck advises that Joe de-triangulate himself. When issues such as the graduation parties come up, Joe must let the children know that Cindy's input will be sought. Joe should respond with something like: "Let me check with my wife." If, for example, Joe and Cindy jointly decide that such extravagance is not feasible, Joe then needs to be careful that he does not tell the children that Cindy will not let him have the money. The response needs to be presented as a united decision: "That is not something that we can do right now."

Roseanne Elling adds,

> Stepfamilies and blended families have so many touchy issues. In addition to Joe and Cindy's discussing finances in general and specifically, they could possibly agree on an amount they could afford to give his daughter to put toward a graduation party, or whatever she decided to do. It's hard to tell if his daughters are trying to manipulate him, which is very possible, or if they desperately want him in their lives and are resorting to money to find assurance that he cares about them. If a parent is absent from a child's life, he or she will "settle" for material things just to get some kind of commitment from that parent.

If Joe and Cindy can discuss their finances and reach agreement before issues arise, if they can address the trust and respect concerns typical of their personality combination in marriage, and if Joe can let go of the guilt and de-triangulate from his children, they will be able to get beyond the immediate crisis and begin to build a strong and healthy marriage.

What about you? Are there factors in your marriage that are in common with Joe and Cindy's? What can you learn from their situation? If money, trust, and/or children from a first marriage are issues in your marriage, you may also find chapters 7, "Orchestrate Finances," and 12, "Between a Rock and a Hard Place," of help.

Interaction

1. First, the husband needs to tackle his struggle with guilt. He should do this by clearly writing out the actions for which he is guilty. In order to gain forgiveness, he must take each item listed to the Lord in prayer and confess it. We read in 1 John 1:9 that "if we confess our sins, he will forgive our sins, because we can trust God to do what is right. He will cleanse us from all the wrongs we have done."

Once he obtains forgiveness from God, he must go to the parties he has wronged—his ex-wife, his family—and ask their forgiveness for the specific issues. Whether they grant forgiveness is not as important as his asking for it. Coming to his family for forgiveness will validate any feelings they have toward him and may defuse anger. The final step is that he must forgive himself, which is often the hardest aspect of forgiveness. Only after he has dealt with his sins will he be able to focus on the true needs of his children without being motivated by guilt.

2. The husband/father needs to facilitate a family meeting with his daughters, his wife, and himself. The purpose of this meeting is to get him out from between his children and his spouse (and his children from between he and his wife). At the meeting he will advise his children that all future decisions, especially those regarding money, will be made together with Cindy. Therefore, they should not expect an immediate response to their requests.

3. The couple needs to exchange trust for respect. As a Peaceful Phlegmatic, Joe needs respect. When he proves himself to be trustworthy, Cindy will be able to respect him. To make this happen, Joe needs to commit to keeping Cindy fully informed. Additionally, he needs to take his place as the spiritual leader in the home. As he gets right with the Lord, his temptation to hide things—in essence, lying—will be displaced by his active relationship with God. Chuck has found that a wife's desire for her husband to be an active spiritual leader in the home is common. With Joe's background as a pastor, this should be an area of strength, and one that he has probably been neglecting. When working to eradicate a bad behavior, it is easier if it is replaced with a good one. In this case, the deception is replaced with spiritual leadership.

4. The wife has been focusing on her husband's weaknesses. As a result, he has been distancing himself from her to the point of hiding things. The wife needs to begin to shift her focus from what is wrong with her husband to what is right. She should start by writing down what originally attracted her to him. Once she has

become more conscious of his good qualities, she needs to look for them on a daily basis and praise him when those qualities are evident. As he begins to make changes for the better, she needs to actively identify what is right and praise him for it. This is where a basic understanding of the Personalities will be especially valuable. The husband's Personality will respond better to praise than to criticism.

3

EX-SPOUSE
ISSUES

Chapter
TEN

An Excess of Ex's

External, Temporary Stress; Ministry

The Issue

*I*t is the second marriage for Jim and for Jayne. They each had been married twenty-three years before and now have been married for nine years. They have discussed many areas of a second marriage, but not what they would do if one of their ex-spouses became seriously ill and would die. They are now faced with that issue.

Jim's ex-wife is dying of cancer and probably has only a couple of months to live. She is not a Christian and has put the responsibility of all of the decisions about dying and what to do on her older son, a young adult. Jim is struggling with how to help his son without sounding as if he is telling him what to do. The marriage problems with his first wife originally revolved around Jim's faith. He is a devoted Christian and she didn't want anything to do with it. In the meantime the son wants to do the right thing, but he is in a dilemma as to what that would be.

Jayne, a Christian, observes the situation from the sidelines, which is difficult for her take-charge Powerful Choleric Personality. She wants to help and support both her stepsons—without making them feel that she is mothering them—to let them know she cares. It is hard for them to see Christ's love through Jayne since they are not believers, even though they go to church.

Additionally, Jayne wants to minister to her husband. She is sure he is experiencing a loss there, but she doesn't know how to address it. After all, the ex-wife is the mother of his children.

Jim is open to discussing how he feels about her dying. He says it is going to be a loss because she was a part of his life and they brought two boys into this world together. However, he does not have any personal feelings about her because that was in the past and those feelings died a long time ago.

Jim and Jayne both want the sons and the grandchildren to know how much they love them. Jim knows what a loss it will be for his boys as he lost his father at any early age. Yet as the stepmother, Jayne doesn't know how to deal with the children and grandchildren. Does she say anything to the grandchildren of five and three about their grandmother—that she will not be in heaven because she is not a believer?

At the same time, Jayne's ex-husband's wife has contacted her. Jayne's ex-husband has committed adultery once again. His wife is not a believer and she is very bitter and angry about what has happened. While Jayne feels compassion for this woman, she doesn't feel it is her problem.

Jim and Jayne discussed many things prior to their marriage, but neither ever thought of these complications. Each feels stressed by circumstances that are totally out of their control. Jim and Jayne feel that God put them together and they were to have the best marriage ever. They'd like to run away from the Issues, which may mean running away from each other.

Insights

The story of Jim and Jayne has a lot going on that most people in a second marriage don't think about. It is easy to be so absorbed in your own issues and the immediate struggles of making the marriage work that you do not think about the "what ifs." This situation brings the reality of those things to light. While there are several concerns at work here, the key issues involve how the current spouse feels. As Jim and Jayne are the ones currently married, their marriage must take priority. As a loving, caring, and Christian individual, Jayne can be a comfort to both of the other women in this scenario, but only as much as Jim feels is appropriate and only if her involvement is not a stress on their marriage.

EX-TERNAL STRESS
The best thing for Jim and Jayne to keep in mind is that the stresses they face now are both external, meaning they are not created within the marriage. They also are not eternal but temporal.

Jim's ex-wife is dying. This is a concern that will not last forever. The question is how Jim and Jayne will handle it. Will it be a growth experience or one that will create resentment for years to come? The crisis of Jayne's ex-husband's wife's trauma will move on as well.

Georgia Shaffer, Pennsylvania-licensed psychologist and author of *A Gift of Mourning Glories*, suggests Jim continue to keep the lines of communication open with Jayne.

> Grieving begins with the loss of his ex-wife's health and will continue for months after her death. It could take years until Jim, his children, and grandchildren fully adjust and rebuild. In the meantime, Jayne must remind herself that grieving is not a situation that can be fixed but a process to be worked through. Jayne needs to give Jim permission to grieve over the loss of his children's mother and realize that intense feelings of sadness and anger can be a part of it.
>
> Jayne also needs to be reminded that the reason grieving lasts far longer than most of us expect is because we can only handle a small amount of pain at a time. Like opening the lid and letting the pressure off a shaken bottle of soda and then closing it, Jim will have times when the death of his wife will be real and painful, and then he will have times when it doesn't affect his day at all. But slowly over time Jim will come to the place of accepting that the mother of his children will no longer be involved in their lives.

Eva Marie agrees. In remembering the death of her ex-husband she says,

> John and I didn't have children, but we had pledged our love and lives to one another in front of God. I believe that forms a soul-tie. Even though the courts separated us, there would always be a thread that kept us together.

First, Jayne needs to take her husband's welfare into consideration. She should be supportive of his feelings of loss and grief. This is not the time for Jayne to feel threatened by the ex-wife—even if she has been in the past. The ex-wife won't be an issue in the future unless Jayne's attitude forces her husband to keep his feelings hidden. If she acts defensively, jealous, or threatened, this behavior is apt to signal to Jim that he cannot discuss his ex-wife with Jayne. She needs to openly support the grieving process, giving Jim and his children control of when and how they process their feelings. She should be a good listener and only offer advice when asked. Despite her love and care for them, she'll be an outsider in this situation. If Jayne attempts to limit Jim or his sons' connection with their ex-wife/mother, it might only result in long-term resentment on their parts.

If her advice is asked, she might suggest that Jim's older son get some outside support in the care of his mother. One option is hospice. After reading about Jim and Jayne's situation, Derryn Lowrey, RN, MSN, offered this counsel:

> It is never too early to involve hospice. They need to be involved at a very early stage instead of when the final curtain is about to fall. Death always comes down to the very basic need of physical care—though emotional issues are obviously not to be ignored. However, you can't look beyond physical needs until those are satisfied. Hospice could relieve the stresses and strains of bodily needs and functions. Taking advantage of what they have to offer would lighten the son's load, leaving him and the rest of the family to deal with the other issues—utilizing their energies for the matters where a stranger could not help.

Michelle Holman, MA, LPC, also encourages Jim's son to seek help:

> Whether it is at his church or with others who face losing a parent to cancer, he should have some outside support. This will enable him to make wise decisions not only for his mother, but ones that protect his current family as well.

In looking at the situation with Jim's ex-wife, Jayne needs to ask herself, "What would be the best-case scenario here?" Chuck suggests that Jayne can only win by taking the high road. While the facts given don't allude to it, one can assume that there is bound to have been some contention between Jayne and the ex-wife. At the least, their disagreement may have to do with their faith. On the other extreme, they may have battled over holidays, alimony, and custody.

Chuck suggests that the optimum outcome might be for Jim's ex-wife to give Jayne her blessing, to say to the children and grandchildren, "I want you to know, you have my blessing to make Jayne *the* grandmother for your children. Please know that you can go to her in times of need. Jayne and I are at peace and we want you to be as well."

With this as a goal, Jayne should start by sharing her concerns with Jim and ask his permission to visit his ex-wife. Assuming this is acceptable, Jayne's aim is to bury the hatchet and offer to reconcile. Being the stronger person, at least spiritually, Jayne must start by apologizing for anything negative that may have gone on between them. Even if the ex-wife is clearly more at fault, Jayne has nothing to gain by holding out. Hopefully the ex-wife will turn around and apologize as well. But if she doesn't, Jayne will have the peace of knowing that she has done the right thing. Georgia Shaffer, author of *A Gift of Mourning Glories*, says,

> Jayne can also serve and support her husband's ex by asking if there are any letters or small gifts she could think to leave behind. Jayne could gather writing paper,

assist with the letter writing, or purchase a few special mementos. Any small thing that would help ease the final separation for her family would be a real gift to them. Unfortunately, Jayne may also have to put her social life on hold during this difficult time. Dinner parties, weekend trips may have to be postponed. When one person has cancer, it affects the lives of all involved. If Jayne can compassionately endure these short-term losses, her marriage will become something even better.

Audrey faced a similar situation: her husband's ex-wife is dying, though the children are younger. She has become friends with this woman and helps out in any way she can. She says,

> I am a friend to the children, but I do not try to mother them. I am sure when she dies the children will be able to come to me for comfort and support. If my neighbor were sick, I would do the same for her. Why should it be any different just because she is my husband's ex-wife?

If Jayne's first efforts are received positively, she might ask the ex-wife if there are any dreams for her children or grandchildren that Jayne can help fulfill. The dying mother may have always wanted to see her son go to law school or to have her grandchild take piano lessons. It could be a comfort to Jim's ex-wife to know that Jayne would be willing to encourage the son by working in his business while he takes time off to pursue his law degree. To help facilitate the grandchild's piano lessons, Jayne might agree that when he is old enough, she will pick him up from school, take him to and from his lessons, listen to him practice, and attend his recitals. Some of the estate could be set aside to help achieve these goals.

POTENTIAL MINISTRY

With Jim's permission and the success of these preliminary steps, Jayne could share Christ with her new friend. However, this may be a place better filled by Jim. Eva Marie shares,

> If I were Jim, I would contact the ex and ask for the opportunity to talk with her. This is where I failed. The Lord spoke to my heart four years before my ex died. He told me that my ex was dying and that I needed to call him. I refused to call. When I got the word that John had died, I grieved as much for my stupidity as for his loss and the loss of his family.

Melanie Wilson, Ph.D., suggests that Jim and Jayne reach out in any way the ex-wife is willing to let them, including taking her into their home.

Her soul is what is important now; love and self sacrificing are the best witnessing tools.

Whether or not she responds favorably to Jayne's witness must not influence the positive relationship Jayne has worked to develop with her.

Additionally, as the outsider, it is not Jayne's place to tell any of the family members that their mother/grandmother is hell-bound. Michelle Holman agrees. She says,

> It is not constructive to tell the grandchildren that their grandmother is going to hell. Instead, continue to encourage and model an authentic relationship with Jesus for them. Let them see the difference He can make in a life.

Melanie Wilson adds,

> I would never tell children or grandchildren that someone beloved is not going to heaven. That is cruel and inappropriate. The fact is, we do not know with absolute certainty the status of anyone's soul.

Georgia Shaffer reminds Jayne to be careful to preserve any precious memories that the children or grandchildren may have:

> To make any unfavorable statements about their mother/grandmother would be detrimental to their emotional well-being.

Sherrie shares what happened in a similar situation when her stepchildren's grandmother passed away.

> Bob's boys' unsaved grandmother passed away. Their mom, Bob's ex, asked us to pray for her, and when she died family members referred to her as being in a "better place." The boys were old enough to figure out that their grandmother didn't profess Jesus as Lord and probably wasn't in heaven. But they didn't and couldn't accept the weight of that likelihood so we never discussed it. Bob and I figured they would come to some determination about that when they were mature enough to consider it fully. At any rate, had we "informed" them, it would have added cruel weight to their loss. To inform anyone of their loved one's eternal destiny is walking on shaky ground, especially children of such young age. Children don't have the ability to process that concept of God's nature—justice. I would advise Jayne to continue to reinforce that God loves their grandmother very much and offer to pray for her with them.

While there is no way to ensure success, one hopes Jayne's actions will result in both women being at peace with each other. This will free the children to develop an ongoing relationship with Jayne without feeling that they are being disloyal to their dead mother.

VICTIMS OF ADULTERY

Audrey mentioned looking at what one might do if a neighbor was facing a difficult time. With this in mind, we look at the situation of Jayne's ex-husband's new wife. Unless Jayne has had an ongoing relationship with her, Jayne is under no obligation to help out in the situation, and should not, if Jim is threatened by Jayne's involvement. For example, talking with her ex-husband's new wife and discussing his adultery could agitate Jayne's past issues and impact her relationship with Jim. As Jim is her priority, he must be taken into consideration first.

The peers who have provided insights throughout the book had mixed feelings on this issue. Shellie offered her thoughts:

> Outside of a definite word from God that this is *the* time to establish a spiritual relationship with and mentor the new wife, Jayne should not actively pursue this right now. She should not put herself in a mentoring position when her husband and the family need so much of her time, energy, attention, and prayers.

In contrast, Karen sees that

> Jayne has a real opportunity here to make a difference in lives by living and loving with Christ's incomparable love. What an incredible testimony to her faith in Christ when she is able to really transcend the normal human response and reach out to her ex-husband's new wife.

While there is no clear-cut answer to this aspect of the situation, if Jim is okay with Jayne's comforting her ex-husband's wife and she can do it without creating emotional turmoil in her own life and marriage, Jayne should do what she can to help. If someone in her church was facing the same difficulty and Jayne had experience with it, she wouldn't hesitate to get involved. In Scripture we are advised to comfort others:

> He comforts us every time we have trouble, so when others have trouble, we can comfort them with the same comfort God gives us. (2 Corinthians 1:4)

While Jayne seems to be unfairly faced with ex-spouse issues on both sides, as a Christian she needs to look at both of these women as women, not as enemies. Everyone involved needs compassion and understanding. As a Christian, Jayne has an opportunity to love extravagantly, not to get but to give.

Interaction

1. The wife's primary responsibility is to meet her husband's needs. Whatever she does in relation to his ex-wife and his sons needs to be within the range of his wishes. The couple needs to discuss the various options presented within the chapter to see which of the possible situations he would be comfortable with her taking. With his approval, she could meet with each of the family members individually to ask how she can be most helpful to them. If he asks her to stay out of it, she must be content with that option.

2. The wife should read *Roses in December* by Marilyn Heavilin to gain an understanding of how each Personality grieves differently.

3. The family should go to grief therapy to help them work through the stages of grief and the unique aspects of this situation.

4. With her husband, the wife needs to determine what involvement she should or should not have with the wife of her ex-husband.

Chapter
ELEVEN

Can't See the Trees
for the Forest

Financial Agreements, Attitude Adjustments, Guilt

The Issue

*D*arren and Louise have been married for about eight years. As a part of his divorce settlement, he agreed to pay his former wife half of what his annual income was then for as long as she lives. At the time, Darren was flying high. He had just had his best year ever. His commitment to his ex-wife is more than many entire families live on—$3000 every month.

However, his industry has faced severe setbacks and Darren's income is not what it once was. The settlement did not allow for any changes in his income. While some might think there should have been a decreasing clause or that she should become independent of him, no such provisions were made. Darren felt sorry for her and feels guilty for divorcing her.

While Darren's current income is adequate to support him, it is not enough to support both him and Louise—let alone his ex-wife. Louise is a hard worker and expected to work when she married Darren, even though his income was higher when they got married. However, Louise has grown weary of the situation. She feels that she must work as hard as she does just to pay the ex-wife—who lives alone and does not work and has no car to maintain. Darren and Louise's expenses vary greatly from hers. Louise feels it is unfair that the ex-wife can live at this comfortable level while she and Darren have to watch their budget closely.

Darren has no intention of reopening this issue in court. In fact, at the time of the divorce he did not have an attorney represent him. He wanted to get it over with and so gave her the house, the car (later sold), and half of his present income for life.

Louise has learned not to bring up this delicate subject. Sometimes she's pretty good about accepting the situation; other times she deeply resents this financial agreement. Louise is doing her best to leave it with God, but it's *hard*! She can't see the trees for the forest.

Insights

Payments to ex-spouses is a volatile issue, and your view may depend heavily on which side of the question your experience lies. Some may quickly jump to the side of Darren's ex-wife, believing that she deserves anything she can get because Darren broke his promise to her by divorcing her. In that case, Louise has no grounds for complaint.

On the flip side, we do not know the circumstances of the divorce. We do know from the information provided that Darren feels guilty for divorcing his ex-wife. It is possible that he is a man of principle and, despite all the things that may have played into the divorce, he feels responsible. By today's standards, Darren's monthly payments are high and providing them for life is uncommon. If the payer's income changes, payments are often adjusted, up or down.

Without complete details about the divorce, the response of either party might be appropriate, so we have chosen to look at both sides as possible options.

If Chuck were seeing Darren and Louise as clients, he would meet with them individually to see who might be more receptive to changing their position, as a resolution will require some compromise. In most relationships, one party is more willing to be flexible and to give, while the other is more resistant to change. The scenario suggests that Louise has accepted her need to adjust and that Darren "has no intention of reopening the issue in court," making him the more rigid. However, in your situation, the tables could be turned. So in order to make this situation beneficial to the most couples, we will address each side as if it were the one to yield. When each spouse is prepared to be the one to change, a compromise is easier to reach. A good premise to work from is the "change first principle": each person takes responsibility for change, regardless of what the other person does. Conversely, it is human nature to meet halfway, which often results in a stalemate.

ATTITUDE ADJUSTMENT

Louise has apparently discussed her feelings with Darren and found that he is unwilling to make an adjustment. So she will have to be the one willing to flex. This process may involve adjusting her attitude about her husband, his responsibility in the situation, and the money.

If Louise is to fully apply the love extravagantly principle in this situation, she will continue to work at "going along with it." After all, she did marry Darren knowing the circumstances and knowing that she would have to contribute financially to their union. Stephanie had to deal with similar issues when she married Kurt. She reports,

> He had an agreement to pay his ex-wife approximately $75,000 over a six-year period. When we married he had five years to go. However, due to his alcohol problem and debts, he became delinquent. The payments went into arrears and it seemed like forever until we were out from under this burden. Yes, we lived on a strict budget, and yes, she bought cars and other things we didn't get. The first thing I had to realize is that when you marry someone, there is no "his debt" or "her debt"—everything is one.

If Louise's heart attitude is to give, not to get—to love extravagantly—where the money she contributes to the checking account actually goes will be a non-issue. However, in day-to-day living that is more easily said than done. As Louise has indicated, some days she does well with it, other days she finds resentment taking over. Here are some practical suggestions to help her make this adjustment:

Several contributors suggested that Louise focus on the good things about Darren. Kristi encouraged Louise to focus on the really important issues, instead of the money:

> Ask yourself, "What genuinely good characteristics is he exhibiting in this situation?" He is a man of integrity who does what he agreed to do. He is a man of loyalty who refused to fight it out in court. He is a man of honor who has no intention of drumming up the unpleasant past. You wouldn't be happy at all if he were stingy, unethical, or cruel. Concentrating on those genuinely fine characteristics instead of the negatives will help you maintain a positive attitude.

Melanie Wilson, Ph.D., agrees. She says,

> It appears that you married a passive, Peaceful Phlegmatic man. Although his failure to stand up to his ex-wife causes you some financial and emotional discomfort, you must have found his personality attractive in many ways. How does his

easygoing personality benefit you? Would you be upset if he suddenly became more controlling and decided to contest the divorce settlement? If he also started to control you, telling you to get a better-paying job? Focusing on his strengths and realizing that the total package is well worth the difficulties may help.

Georgia Shaffer, Pennsylvania-licensed psychologist, suggests that not only does Louise need to refocus on Darren's positive attributes, she also needs to ignore the lifestyle of Darren's ex-wife.

On those on days when things are going especially well for Louise, she could create a gratitude list of those gifts she has received as a result of being married. For example, if Louise were single a greater percentage of her income would be going to the essential costs of living such as housing, electricity, and telephone. The fact that Darren contributes anything to these expenses provides her with a better lifestyle. On those days when she is tired and the ex-wife issue resurfaces, Louise can reread her gratitude list and be reminded of what is good in her life.

So Louise could start by adjusting her attitude about Darren. Next she may need to learn to accept the situation as it is. Kathy writes,

In this case, the second wife really has no grounds for complaint. Her husband was then the husband of the first wife. The guilt he felt was justified—he divorced her. The commitment he gave her is the consequence of divorce. Similar to the old adage, "Ignorance of the law is no excuse," the breakup of a marriage always has consequences—whether we like it or not. Darren is honoring his word and that is commendable.

Stephanie adds,

I found peace when I was able to accept that divorce is not of God and we must face some hard knocks as a result of those choices.

The harsh reality is, there are consequences of divorce and Louise did know about them heading into her marriage with Darren. As a result, it is not reasonable for her to expect him to make changes now because she is unhappy with the arrangement. As others have pointed out, Darren is an honorable man to hold to his agreement—which is something few do today. So Louise should focus on Darren's strengths and accept her situation. Additionally, she may need to change her view of the money, as Karen suggests.

As both an ex-wife and the new wife, Karen says,

I think she truly has no option but to honor her husband by accepting his choice.

She cannot control it, so she must try to see it differently in order to not harbor resentment. Perhaps she can change her way of thinking. Pretend the money is an unavoidable expense [which it really is], like a health issue. Her effort to accept his decision will pay off in the long run because he will ultimately appreciate her acceptance of his decision.

Along the same lines, Melanie Wilson asks,

What if you decided not to even think about the money going to his ex-spouse? You just tell yourself that your husband's income is complete with his portion. When you find yourself tempted to be concerned about the ex-wife's spending or lifestyle, remind yourself that it is none of your business. Instead, God would have you focus on your own stewardship.

Chuck would advise Louise and Darren to adjust their lifestyle to be able to easily live on Darren's remaining income, whatever that may be, combined with Louise's. If that is not sufficient, perhaps Darren could take on an additional part-time job or do some consulting work on the side so both feel that he is "providing." Additionally, seeing Darren making this extra effort may help Louise feel that she is not alone in her hard work and income production.

These suggestions can help Louise deal with the practical aspects of her situation. Additionally, there is a spiritual element that must be addressed. Like Louise, many of us become so focused on the Issue—the trees—that we can't see the bigger picture, the forest. But God sees the whole thing.

Kristi reminds Louise to focus on the Lord.

[God] is your real resource for life, not your salary or your husband's. He can provide more than enough for both households.

Stephanie continues,

This has nothing to do with Louise. In a loving way, she needs to tell Darren her deepest fears and resentments. She needs to realize that he made a commitment and she must help him honor it. God supplies all our needs, and we somehow think we always deserve more.

In the Bible study I attend, we were recently talking about God's provision for us. The question came up, "How has God provided for you in a time of need?" I thought of a year ago when Chuck's employment situation was in turmoil and just making the house payment was a struggle. God did supply, though not in the way

I would have chosen. Over a period of a few months I was involved in four minor traffic accidents. Two were my fault. Two were not. My vehicle was not damaged to the point that it had to be repaired to drive, but it was damaged. I received checks from the insurance companies that made a big difference at the time. Miraculously, our insurance was never cancelled! Since that time, our life has stabilized—as has my driving. It has been months since I've had an accident, and Chuck and I are planning on fixing my car's smashed front end soon.

Matthew 6:25–34 is a good reminder of God's provision for all of us. Louise might want to focus on verse 33:

> The thing you should want most is God's kingdom and doing what God wants. Then all these other things you need will be given to you.

While this will be hard for Louise, she can make these adjustments. After all, her marriage is more important than worrying about rights or keeping a fairness tally. That is the whole goal of loving extravagantly—not to get, but to give.

GUIDED BY GUILT

While it is easy to point a finger at Louise with a you-asked-for-it-you-got-it attitude, there is another side to the story. Chuck would like to talk to Darren about his duty to his current marriage to Louise. Did guilt rather than logic, the law, or even reason guide the marital separation agreement?

Addressing her approach to this situation, Michelle Holman, MA, LPC, says,

> I would talk to Darren about praying toward God leading them to a reasonable resolution. I would also ask him to pray that God would reveal any guilt about the divorce associated with his financial support. Often when a spouse just gives in to the other spouse, it is their way of not acknowledging the reality of a failed marriage—which, especially for Christians, is a grief process and takes time and a lot of grace.

Divorce is not God's perfect plan. Yes, it is a sin. Yes, it does have consequences. But the wonderful thing about God is his grace. Assuming that Darren has asked for God's forgiveness for his role in the divorce, he is forgiven. His life does not need to be ruled by guilt. In addressing divorce and remarriage, the notes in my *Women's Study Bible* say,

> With God, forgiveness is as if it never happened. No sin or tragedy is beyond God's forgiveness. After seeking God's forgiveness, which we all do repeatedly, a woman [man] who remarries has a new understanding of God's incredible grace.[1]

Darren appears to have made a choice based on guilt. While some support may be in order as a consequence, Darren's settlement does appear to be outside the norm, especially today. CPA Reese Gateley says,

> From the financial side, I have never seen an agreement like the one you are describing. Darren has boxed himself into a corner. He never should have represented himself. Guilt [apparently] took over.

Michelle Holman agrees:

> Some states do not even make allowances for alimony. . . . It's usually only given if the wife has been a stay-at-home mom and needs time to prepare for a career.

Since we believe Darren is a Peaceful Phlegmatic, we can assume that he may be taking the path of least resistance—choosing peace now while putting off any conflict that would result in long-term contentment. As his therapist, Chuck would confront him with the reality of the situation, telling him, "That's $36,000 a year, $360,000 every ten years. Is that what you want to do?" If Darren hasn't thought this through, Chuck would coach him to take responsibility for doing what's best for the long term—taking care of Louise—and to do it now rather than putting off the unpleasant task. The longer he waits, the deeper the hole. More resentment will build in Louise, and the ex-wife's expectation of ongoing support will be more firmly entrenched.

Chuck would also press for an answer to the question, "Is this fair to Louise? If you were single, without the benefit of Louise's income, would you be able to pay your ex-wife and still live?" Perhaps this reality would help Darren see the situation from Louise's point of view and make him willing to look into making an adjustment.

From this perspective, Chuck would encourage Darren and Louise to talk to a lawyer who has expertise in these issues in their state—not committing to any change, but to investigate their options. A lawyer may review the case and determine that there is no choice. At this point, the issue would be closed and not pursued further. But Louise would feel valued knowing that Darren cared enough to seek to make a change, which should help her to adjust her attitude, even if no change in the agreement can be made.

If a change is possible, then Darren and Louise will need to spend time in prayer and seek wise counsel as to their next course of action. Making a change is something that can only be determined between them and God. Darren may want to consider the fact that if he and his first wife had never divorced, she would have had to make adjustments when his income changed.

Chuck would then meet with Darren and Louise as a couple. He would have each affirm the other's position in mutual submission (Ephesians 5:21). The Bible asks husbands and wives to submit to one another out of reverence for Christ—that is, each giving 100 percent. Louise would say, "I married you debts and all, and I support you in your commitment to honor your ex-wife." Darren would say to Louise, "I realize I was driven by guilt and have taken the easy path. This has placed an unfair burden on you as my wife. My duty is to do what is best for you now." When each person is willing to go more than half way, it lays the groundwork for a healthy compromise. This takes maturity on the part of both spouses. In his book *Sacred Marriage*, Gary Thomas says,

> A mature husband and wife can grow leaps and bounds spiritually as they learn to compromise and move toward the other.[2]

If they do decide to proceed with an adjustment in the settlement, Darren and his ex-wife must agree to a change, or they will need to go back to court—which is likely. If Darren is willing to reopen the issue, legal counsel should definitely be sought.

Ideally both Darren and Louise would be willing to let go a little and meet in the middle. In their case, that might mean doing what it takes to make a reasonable adjustment to the marital settlement agreement. If Darren remains resolute, Louise can still make adjustments to her attitude that will make a big difference in their relationship—this is true extravagant love, selfless love, and although it feels like being lost in the trees, it is God's view of the entire forest.

If you find other financial or related issues cropping up in your marriage, the situations in section 2, "Financial Issues," will also be of help.

The Interaction

FOR THE HUSBAND:

1. Write ten different statements describing why you feel guilty for having divorced your ex-wife.

2. Evaluate each of the guilt statements. Address whether each one does or does not constitute a legitimate source of guilt *in the present*. For each current source of guilt, write why it is legitimate.

3. Then for each source of legitimate guilt, write a response to the following:

- Have I asked God for forgiveness? Has he forgiven me?

- Have I forgiven myself?
- Have I asked my ex-wife for forgiveness?
- I can gain forgiveness by _____.

4. Write a response either agreeing or disagreeing with the following statements:
   - Giving money to my ex-wife will earn forgiveness.
   - My duty is to my current wife.

FOR THE WIFE:

1. Write ten reasons why excessive payments to the ex-wife would reasonably build resentment in you. (This is to begin validating your feelings.)

2. Write down your fears for the present and future. Evaluate each for probability. Share your feelings with your spouse.

3. Write a marital balance sheet, using the format an accountant would use, with the alimony payment as a debit or loss. List on one side all the things that are good in the marriage (assets), both financial and otherwise. An asset might be something as simple as "We have fun together" or "He makes me laugh." On the other side, list all the things that are negative (liabilities). Ideally, this will help put the liability of the alimony in perspective. (If this were a premarital situation, this exercise would help determine if the relationship should continue.)

4. List the things you are asking your husband to do before you can accept the payments to the ex-wife as a business expense with no emotion attached to it. (For example: See lawyer to look into reduced payments.)

5. List the things you can do in the event your husband makes no changes.

4

STEPFAMILY ISSUES

Chapter TWELVE

Between a Rock and a Hard Place

Discipline, Commitment

The Issue

When Ben and Lucille began dating, she was a widow with two children—a daughter, Nancy, who was in high school and a son, Billy, who was in junior high. Ben included the children in their dates. Though he'd been warned of a possible tug-of-war for their mother's affections, Ben felt up to the challenge and he didn't hesitate to spend a lot of time with them. On weekends, he frequently took them all on a drive to a location where they could picnic, fish, or take a walk in nature. Many times the day ended with a barbecue.

Ben knew that Lucille's first husband, the father of her children, was abusive and that Lucille and the children still harbored fears from their traumatic experiences. If Ben raised his voice, the children quickly moved toward their mother, as if to protect her. As he continually demonstrated love and consistency—though not perfect—he gently wooed them; their fears seemed to evaporate. He tried to use every opportunity to demonstrate to them what a man who loved them should be like. He believed love would conquer all.

Soon after the couple's wedding, Ben started noticing changes in Billy, who flew into a rage when corrected, daring Ben to discipline him—shouting, "You're not my father! You can't tell me what to do!" Although Ben and Lucille differed on what should be done, they did what they could to calm and redirect him, but he kept on making wrong choices. Ben held a firm hand and Lucille was more lax. One day the call came from the sheriff that he had Billy in custody and was taking him to juvenile hall.

Arguments between Ben and Lucille about how to deal with Billy have escalated. Ben has begun to wonder if they wouldn't all be better off if he left the marriage. After all, if he stays and can't do anything to stop Billy's waywardness, Ben feels he would be blamed for not doing what he could. But if he leaves, he would be leaving Lucille, whom he loves. He can't stay and he can't go. Each day seems worse. Ben is stuck between a rock and a hard place.

Insights

While Ben and Lucille's situation does have some complications that make it unique, they also have concerns, struggles, and frustrations that are common to households where two adults with different approaches to discipline live and where teenagers are present. Regardless of the past issues, it is imperative that Ben and Lucille present a united front. Rebellion in teenagers is a problem that many parents face. Ben has become a stabilizing factor in Billy's life, and his departure could create additional problems for Billy. Ben needs to honor his commitment.

UNITED FRONT

Our scenario indicates that Ben has come into a home accustomed to turbulence and he has a grounding effect: "As he gently wooed them, the fears seems to evaporate." However, shortly after Ben and Lucille were married, things began to change between Ben and Billy. Ben is making assumptions that Billy resents his presence and that things are getting worse. Although one can clearly see how Ben might jump to this conclusion, Ben needs to remember that Billy brought plenty of his own emotional issues into this new relationship. Michelle Holman, MA, LPC, sees that this behavior is typical of Billy's situation. She explains,

One problem that I see over and over again is when a parent has over-bonded with a child because of an absent or abusive spouse. When a new marriage/relationship presents, the child is angry, resentful, and/or jealous of the new connection and doesn't know how to adjust.

This may be the case with Lucille and Billy. For many years she may have had to protect him from his father. Now that he is older, she doesn't know how to make the adjustment from protecting him to disciplining him. Additionally, in situations when a child loses a parent, he tends to become very possessive of the remaining parent. Anyone new in the home, such as Ben, is bound to generate anxiety. The existing equilibrium is being temporarily thrown off balance.

We might also assume from the case presented that Ben probably has the stronger Personality and that Lucille is apt to be the more passive of the two. If this is the case, it might be easy for Lucille to give the reins of discipline to Ben— the male. However, that will split the desirable structure of the family. Ben will be above Lucille and the children. Instead, Lucille and Ben need to be peers together in authority above the children. Because Lucille was previously in the role of protector, it is especially important that her children see her and Ben as working together.

Contributors Ruth and Bill believe that their joining together to deal with her son Jim's anger is central to their success with him. Like Ben, Bill made the decision as to how things should be done, but Ruth totally supported his choice. Looking back on that time, Ruth remembers,

> Jim's relationship with Bill was very similar to Billy's with Ben—defiance, anger, rejection. We didn't get into police and juvenile hall issues, but I believe that would have happened if Bill and I had not handled things as we did. God gave me the grace to get out of the way and allow Bill to deal with Jim as he believed he should. I backed him up in his decisions about Jim. I did not run interference for either of them.

Ruth reports that today Jim is grown up—self-supporting and self-sufficient.

> Jim calls Bill "Dad" at least part of the time (his choice), asks him for advice (and sometimes even follows it), turns to him for praise and affirmation, and in general accepts him as his father.

Susan Rogers, MA, LPC, advises parents and stepparents, saying,

> It is helpful for the stepmother to say, "These are your dad's rules and I am supporting his wishes." The stepfather can say, "These are your mother's rules and I am supporting her wishes." This keeps the inevitable argument that "You're not my real parent" at bay.

Additionally, it is not healthy for Lucille's daughter, Nancy—or Billy—to think that only men have power. Lucille must share in the disciplinary action, providing a healthy model for the children to internalize. Avoiding it will set Ben up as the "bad cop"—increasing the children's anger and resentment toward him. While good cop/bad cop may work in interrogating criminals, it is a bad model for raising children.

Bev grew up in a situation similar to that of Ben and Lucille. Her brother also had trouble with the law. Her mother was hesitant to come down hard on her brother; after all, he had been through so much: an alcoholic father, desertion, and divorce. By the time Bev's stepfather arrived on the scene, many of the family's behavior patterns were firmly established. He had an uphill battle trying to set boundaries for Bev's brother, especially without Bev's mother's support. Bev reports,

> My mom and stepdad met with a probation officer on a regular basis. My mom gave my stepdad more and more freedom in dealing with my little brother. She could see that her approach was not doing the job. At first my brother was even worse in his behavior at home. He showed his hatred of my stepdad for depriving him of his freedoms when he disobeyed. But, with my mom's support, my stepfather held firm and steady.
>
> It took months, but like a ship being turned by a tug, my brother started changing his behavior. By the end of the year, my brother was making different choices most of the time. My mom followed the lead my stepfather set and stood with him in making my brother accountable. I'd encourage Lucille to do the same.

Georgia Shaffer, Pennsylvania-licensed psychologist, agrees:

> So often we grow weary when the situation we are attempting to improve isn't fixed immediately. We gave it our best and quickly conclude that our best wasn't good enough. Billy's problems are a result of many difficult years, and in order to make a lasting change it will likely take much longer than Ben and Lucille have the patience for. They need to continue providing a loving, supportive, and structured environment and focus on God's ability to transform the most hopeless of circumstances.

Chuck sees it as imperative that Ben and Lucille speak with one voice and offers Ben encouragement:

> Sometimes when kids finally get into a safe environment, they begin to act out unresolved issues—which need to come out eventually. Billy's behavior could be because he is feeling safe for the first time in his childhood.

Billy is bound to have issues with grief, abandonment, and anger. Since the biological father is no longer present, Billy is projecting his feelings about his father onto Ben. In counseling, Chuck has often been the target of a child's anger that was really about, and originated with, his father. Once in a therapeutic setting, the child feels safe expressing these previously pent up emotions.

Having been through something very similar, Jan found this was true with her daughters. She explains that their father's abandonment and his starting a new family with someone else traumatized her two "prodigal teenage daughters."

> They were acting out their anger in the only safe place they had—me. They resisted every man who came around. It took many years and much firm patience on my part for them to heal.

Richard had similar difficulties with his own son:

> My son lived with his mother until she threw him out when he was thirteen. She had him move in with a friend of hers who put him into counseling and encouraged him to face his problems. In November of that year, the friend called us to say that she could no longer keep him. My new wife and I would have to try to raise him. We struggled to help him and keep him on the right course—but being his father's son, he had to learn everything the hard way. I was tempted to kick him out many times, and I had plenty of reasons: a DWI at age sixteen, drugs, getting a girl pregnant. . . . However, every time I was ready to give up, I was reminded by God that what he needed was love. Together my wife and I worked to love this unlovable teenager until he finally did graduate from high school and move out.

Ben and Lucille must stand shoulder to shoulder in their agreed-upon discipline and their love for Billy. The boundaries they give Billy are a form of love. While working with violent offenders in a residential treatment center, Chuck found that even violent teens are fearful of an environment where there is no order or control and ultimately respond positively to healthy boundaries.

Finding the balance between showing Billy that he is loved and giving him boundaries is a difficult task. A good approach is to give Billy as much freedom as his ability to handle responsibility allows. If his actions continue to indicate that he cannot be trusted with responsibility, then his freedoms need to be pulled in, tightening the reins.

I remember my rebellious teen years. Every time I went too far, every time I messed up, some of my freedoms were taken away. It wasn't that I was grounded or specifically punished—depending on the violation—but next time I asked for permission for something that was questionable, the freedom was denied. If my failures were few and far between, the restrictions on my freedoms were minimal or nonexistent. If they were frequent, the boundaries were moved in tighter. I understood this system and often knew that a certain choice would cost me many weeks of earning back my parents' trust.

While not a stepparent herself, Mary Hunt Webb, MA, has faced similar circumstances in the classroom as a college educator. Mary says,

> Billy is looking for boundaries, and as a result, he is crashing into them all the time. He must be shown that the boundaries are there and that they will not dissolve—no matter what he does. In situations like this, it is good if Billy can receive consequences for his actions from sources outside the home. This way, Billy would not see the consequences as Ben and Lucille's punishing him; it would be society telling him that this kind of behavior is not acceptable. It would be easy for Lucille to continue trying to protect him, this time from the punishment of the law. But she and Ben must stand together and allow the law to give Billy a wake-up call.

Melissa was also having big problems with her two teenage sons. She shared,

> I tended to be a "bail-out" parent—overcompensating for the divorced and uninterested father who remarried and started over with new kids. A psychologist I saw during that time told me that "we all have to stop mothering at some point in time. The natural progression of the relationship is from parent/child to adult/adult, and everyone hits it at different times in their life." For me, because of my younger son's constant trouble with the law, I was told to *stop* mothering and let the consequences hit him hard, as they were deserved. She said, "Law-breakers are sometimes created because they never feel the consequences early in life. They keep pushing the barriers and ultimately decide there is no reason not to do whatever suits them."

Psychotherapist Michelle Holman suggests,

> Ben and Lucille can decrease their conflict involving day-to-day family discipline by sitting down with both Billy and Nancy and creating a family constitution and contract as suggested by Gary Smalley and Dr. Greg Smalley in their book *Bound by Honor*.

Assuming that Ben and Lucille can come to a place where they agree on Billy's discipline, their personal arguments should be minimized. Once Ben realizes that Billy's anger is not about him, he can work with it without becoming angry or defensive. Ben indicates that he still loves Lucille, and together they need to face the future.

COMMITMENT

Noted management guru Peter Drucker says, "Unless commitment is made, there are only promises and hopes . . . but no plans." I find that this applies perfectly here. Unless Ben is committed to the marriage, to Lucille and to Billy and Nancy, they have only promises and hope. As an important step in the plan, Ben needs to hang in there.

While that is easier said than done, all those who have responded encourage Ben that it does get better. Billy may be testing him: will the love Ben exhibited and invested during the courtship of his mother last? Will Ben resort to abusive behavior like Billy's father did?

As additional encouragement Chuck likes to point out to stepfathers that if they are the ones bringing up the child, they are the real parents, regardless of blood. The Bible shows a long genealogy for Christ—forty-two generations—leading up to Joseph (Matthew 1:1–17). However, Joseph was not the biological father of Jesus; he was, in effect, his stepfather. Yet Joseph raised him as his own. Nowhere in Scripture does it indicate that Joseph was any less important in the life of Jesus than Mary—whose blood Christ did share. Joseph loved Jesus extravagantly. He didn't do it because Jesus was his bloodline, but because God called him to do it.

The study notes of the *Women's Study Bible* say,

We can learn from Joseph three important qualities for godly stepparents:

- He did what the Lord asked him to do (Matthew 1:24).
- He allowed others to give good things to the child in his care (Matthew 2:11).
- He acted quickly to protect his child (Matthew 2:14–15).[1]

By marrying Lucille, Ben accepted God's call to be Billy's "real" father. Chuck has learned by working with children that to a child, the "real" father is the one who fulfills the role: "He took me to a baseball game, like a real dad." Young children do not distinguish between the father whose seed birthed them and the one who brings them up. However, our adult minds view the "real" dad as the sperm donor. This is something that adults have taught children as a means of positioning. In working with blended families, the concept of real parent versus stepparent is false and needs to be broken. Margorie Engel, president of the Stepfamily Association of America, says,

We still live with the concept that DNA determines a family, rather than who does the nurturing.[2]

It is human nature to favor your own bloodline. Loving extravagantly allows

God's nature to dominate by becoming the real father to the children he has placed in your care. With this in mind, when Billy acts out, telling Ben, "You are not my real father!" Ben needs to respond with extravagant love by saying, "You are my real son." This addresses the true emotional need of Billy rather than being caught up in a power struggle.

To help develop a parent/child relationship, Sandy's blended family support group developed a plan for a situation like Ben and Lucille's. She describes the first husband as "abusive, uncaring, and immature."

> The mother was attached to the children in an overprotective way. She married a man with an even temper and a loving personality. The new husband must develop a separate relationship with the children as well as a team relationship with the mom. This is a hard concept for traditional families to understand. The idea is that we must treat the stepchildren as individuals rather than extensions of our spouse or the ex-spouse. This can be one of the hardest ideas to accomplish in a stepfamily. We may often view the stepchild as an interference, a spy, or an opponent. We must see them as individuals whom our spouse loves and cherishes. The real relationship must start from that viewpoint.

In Bev's childhood family, this adjustment was not an easy process. Reflecting on the relationship of her brother and stepfather, she says,

> It was a struggle, but when my brother graduated from high school several years later, he thanked my stepfather for making it possible. He knew he probably would have been in jail if he had continued the way he'd been going. My stepfather had already raised two lovely daughters. It was extremely difficult to try to raise a son who was already half grown. Many times I know he felt like giving up, but he held on. The struggle was worth what was achieved.

As a part of hanging in there and getting Billy on the right path, Michelle Holman encourages Lucille to look at her relationship with Billy:

> She may need to confess any improper emotional relationship she has had with him. A counselor may be needed to help them establish a healthy relationship and to walk with Billy to help him grieve the loss of the over connection. In cases like this the parent has often become a "god" in the eyes of the child. One parent is all good, while the other is all bad.

Georgia Shaffer says,

> Unfortunately over connecting can be found in many single parent families. When

the parent and children together face and endure very difficult times, it is natural to form a strong bond. However, this becomes a problem when the parent continues to rely on the children for emotional support, failing to process the loss and begin anew.

Jan found this was true with her daughters. As a Popular Sanguine, she sought to soothe their hurt by creating "fun" togetherness, especially shopping at the mall.

Trying to be both mother and father, I way overbonded with my girls. Through counseling, I learned it was unhealthy for us. Besides, my budget couldn't take much more. I had to learn to cut the umbilical cord.

Chuck advises Ben to stay the course and ride it out. Leaving will not solve the issues and is apt to make them worse. Mary Hunt Webb points out:

Even without a stepfather in the picture, Billy would be having similar problems as a result of what happened with his birth father. There is a natural tendency to think that Billy is behaving the way he is as a result of having a stepfather, but the teen years can be horrendous—regardless of what the family composition is. Ben is looking for someone to blame for Billy's behavior and has chosen himself as the culprit. If Ben left, Billy would probably be worse. It would cement in his mind that no man can be trusted; that would almost guarantee that both children would have issues in their adult life.

Richard hung in with his son and got him through high school. Bev's stepfather stood firm and held her brother accountable, getting him through high school and finally receiving thanks for his efforts. In his book *Growing Up*, award-winning columnist Russell Baker tells how he resented his stepfather all through his teen years and did nothing to make life easier for him. But when Baker became an adult, things really hit home for him. He realized the sacrifices his stepdad had made.[3] With commitment, Ben can plan to help Billy live out his promise and hope. There is no guarantee that Billy will get through high school, that he will ever thank Ben, or that he will ever truly appreciate all his stepfather has done for him, but Ben needs to make that effort and he needs to make his marriage commitment a priority.

In *Sacred Marriage*, Gary Thomas reminds us that it may not be easy, that some effort is required to make our marriage work:

When we get married, we make a certain promise to our spouse that we will devote a considerable amount of energy, initiative and time into building and nurturing the relationship. . . . When marriage is placed within the context of God's redemptive plan, we stay married.[4]

When Jan and Carl married, both of Jan's daughters were adults, yet they still had trouble accepting him as their stepfather:

> We've had many battles in the last five years. Carl has remained consistent in his love for me and supportive yet firm in our joint family decisions. The girls have come to respect his common sense and now introduce him as their dad. He has been the stabilizing factor we needed.

Gene and Lynn made a commitment to each other when they entered into marriage, the second for both. Gene had three children, thirteen, fifteen, and nineteen, who lived with their mother in a different state. Lynn has two children, thirteen and sixteen. Both lived with her. Gene reports his situation—somewhat like Ben's:

> After we were married, everything was fine—for the first few months. Then teenage rebellion hit. Lynn's son had been "man of the house" since her divorce eight years earlier. Since we married, I had not disciplined either of her children.

One night Gene came home to find Lynn's son giving her a tongue-lashing about something he refused to do.

> I did not interfere in that heated exchange, but the argument continued and the situation escalated. I decided to take action.

Gene reports that he walked in on them and stood nose-to-nose with his stepson. He demanded,

> You will not talk to your mother like that anymore. Do you understand?

With fire in his eyes, Lynn's son informed Gene in no uncertain terms that he was not going to tell him what to do.

> When he shouted, "You are not my dad!" I calmly replied, "Let me say it again. You will not talk to your mother like that anymore. Do you understand?" Then, I turned and walked to the bedroom and closed the door. After a few minutes, there was a knock at the door. He asked if he could come in. I opened the door and was greeted with a hug. With tears streaming down his face, he cried, "I love you. I'm sorry."

Gene and Lynn made a pact based on Mark 10:9: "What God has joined to-gether, let no man separate." Gene says, "That included the children."

The years pass. Teenagers become adults. Relationships heal and grow. Between us we have five children who have blessed us with wonderful grandchildren who will also pass through those teenage years.

For Ben and Lucille, for you and your spouse, we encourage you to stand on that Scripture as well—to love each other extravagantly; not to get, but to give, even if you feel like giving up!

The Interaction

1. Whenever possible, communicate that the direction of one parent reflects the support of the other:

- Mother: "Your father and I have decided _____."
- Father: "Your mother and I have decided _____."

Whenever pressed by the teen, a good fallback position is "Let me check with your mother/father before I give you my decision."

2. Create a log of the child's attempts to split up or divide the parents. This will bring awareness to the family dynamic. For example, Billy might say to Lucille, "Ben tells me stupid stuff to do! Do I really have to sweep the driveway?" Always back up the other parent, even if you think they are wrong! Disagreement and discussion should take place between adults, away from the children. Never let the child rush you into making a decision.

3. The stepfather needs to facilitate the creation of a "dad" name for the stepchild to call him. For example, "Billy, it is important to me that you call me something like "Dad." I know you think of your birth father as "Dad." Is there something else you would be willing to call me, like "Papa" or "Pop?" This gives the child permission to call the stepfather a dad. The stepfather has taken the emotional risk of rejection by taking the initiative here. The selected name should communicate respect while showing endearment. It should not be the parent's first name, nor should it be "Father" or "Sir," as these are too formal.

4. When the child says, "You can't tell me what to do. You're not my real father," respond with, "You're my real son. I can and will tell you what to do." The stepfather needs to refer to his stepson as "son." Place a hand on his shoulder or hug him when appropriate. Healthy touch is very important for teen boys *and* girls.

Emotional Roller Coaster

Security, Healthy Relationships

The Issue

Lila and Dennis have been married for about six years. It is a second marriage for each and they both have children from their previous marriages. Lila's teenage sons live with them and are busy with sports, school, and church activities. Dennis's daughters—who are younger than Lila's sons—are with them every other weekend. Most of the time, she and Dennis have a good relationship and she feels secure in his love. However, the minute his girls walk in the door, they become number one and Lila takes a backseat. She has stood by him through battles with his ex-wife and business struggles, yet when his daughters are present, she questions his love for her.

Dennis complains that Lila would like his daughters to simply disappear, which he says "will never happen," as they will always be a part of his life and they do come first. Lila feels hurt by Dennis' response. She feels tense and stressed the days before the girls arrive. As a result their marriage suffers. Lila snaps unnecessarily at Dennis, and the anger she feels has built up over the six years of their marriage. Lila feels that the more Dennis cares for the girls, the more her resentment builds. Her anger spills out onto his children, pushing them closer and closer to Dennis.

Lila loves the girls, but feels a great sense of relief when they leave. She feels that she is on an emotional roller coaster and wonders what she can do to adjust to this biweekly upheaval.

Insights

Shuttling children back and forth between parents is usually accompanied by complications. Adding a stepparent brings an additional element into the mix that is seldom easy and often results in a variety of problems. Glen T. Stanton, author of *Why Marriage Matters*, states,

> The roles of stepparent and stepchild are hard to define and the emotional attachment of these two parties is quite different from the emotional attachment between a biological or adoptive parent and child.[1]

It is no wonder that Lila is having some difficulties in her relationships with both her husband and her stepdaughters. Each relationship will need work to bring Lila, Dennis, and the girls into a stable and satisfying place. First we will look at Lila's need for security, and then at building a mutually respectful relationship between her and the girls.

SECURITY

Whether or not Lila's feeling of insecurity is warranted, it is a valid feeling and one shared by many women in her place. Sherrie is familiar with Lila's predicament. She writes,

> Lila and Dennis's situation is so painfully familiar. Bob and I have been married for nine years, and we have weathered the storms of blending our family. I look back and see that I was unexplainably insecure.

While Sherrie says she was "unexplainably insecure," Gaylen Larson, Ph.D., sees that as a natural and expected response.

> Because of the way women are wired, they have a deep inner need for security. The number one need in females is for security—both financial and relational; this is seen in what is known as the nesting instinct. Just the fact that she has entered into a new marriage shakes up her equilibrium as she adjusts to her new husband. Adding his children into the picture exacerbates the situation. Men, on the other hand, are wired with a primary need to feel significant and important. On his own Dennis is not likely to see how Lila perceives the situation or understand her need for security.

This need is something that both Lila and Dennis will need to work at.

Rose Sweet is a pastoral counselor and the author of *How to Be First in a Second Marriage*. She says,

Some people would be quick to point a finger at Lila, citing her insecurity and jealous nature. Misguided advice such as "Grow up," "Get over it," "You're the adult," and "You're so insecure" only serve to make the Lilas of the world feel even more rejected and at the bottom of the totem pole.

While there may be some element of truth in the "grow up" statements, they are not the only solution. As Gaylen Larson explained, insecurity is to be expected in this situation. However, realizing the cycle she is in, Lila as an adult needs to take some steps to correct the situation. Sherrie confirms this in her story:

> After years of handling it all wrong, I cried out to God. He gave me some amazingly comforting words—grow up! I had to ask myself who the adults were in our situation.

No matter how valid Lila's feelings are, she cannot expect the girls to "disappear." What she can do, however, is to adjust her expectations. Kathy relates to Lila's frustrations:

> I too felt ambushed by stepchildren. I didn't want them over. I felt that he loved them more than me. What I really was saying is that I *only* want *us*! Twenty years have passed. I regret that I was not more mature at the time.

Susan Rogers, MA, LPC, reminds Lila:

> Dennis' relationship with his daughters precedes his relationship with you by several years. It is understandable that he will have a strong sense of loyalty to them, and this is an admirable fatherly quality.

Understanding this was very helpful to Sherrie in adjusting her attitude. She reports,

> While change did not come overnight, I realized that Bob's children had visiting rights and a schedule long before I came along. It's as though they were playing catch in the proverbial park of life, having found their way together and sharing a survivors' bond. I strolled in out of the blue and said, "Hey, throw me the ball too!" Then I was saying, "No fair. I didn't get a turn." Soon I tried stealing the ball, hiding it, and pouting on the sidelines. Finally, I demanded, "Include me, or else."

While Lila should not beat herself up over her feelings of insecurity, neither should she wallow in them. She needs to adjust her expectations and move on.

Understanding and accepting Dennis' longstanding relationship with his daughters will help her overcome her insecurities. Sherrie tried to put herself in her husband's place to help her adjust her attitude about her husband's children and their relationship.

> I asked myself, "If I were him, what would I want?" As I focused on Bob and thought about how I could serve him, the resentment gave way to love. I realized we would be together long after the kids were all grown and raising kids of their own. Could I not give them this time together?

Ah, the power of extravagant love—not to get, but to give!

In his book *Sacred Marriage*, Gary Thomas encourages slowing down long enough to look at someone else's needs:

> It just may be that God gives us the marriage relationship to moderate and redirect our dreams. Forced to compromise, we learn to reevaluate what's truly important. We are asked to reconsider our priorities and slow down long enough to look at someone else's opinion or needs.[2]

Remembering her own struggles, Pam encourages Lila,

> Sometimes we as second wives forget there are other people in our husband's life. Pray that God will give you insight into how to handle your feelings and the situation. I believe that if you change your attitude, it could change your husband's. We are having the whole crew—my husband's boys, my mom, and my daughter and her husband—over for Thanksgiving. This will be the first time in nine years that both of our children will be with us for a holiday. They are all spending a couple of days with us. God answers prayers and heals the hearts of those who have been hurt so deeply.

As Lila begins to make some changes of her own, hopefully Dennis will change as well—the existing equilibrium will change. First Dennis needs to remember that scripturally he and Lila are one. Genesis 2:24 says, "This explains why a man leaves his father and mother and is joined to his wife, and the two are united into one." (NLT)

With this in mind, Jean Cox-Turner, RN, parent educator, and stepparent herself states:

> Dennis should include Lila in at least some of the activities with his daughters. He should sit down with the girls and tell them how much he loves them and how much he loves Lila. Lila is his wife and he wants them all to be a family.

Susan Rogers advises Dennis:

You can help by reassuring Lila of your love and commitment to make this new family work. Remember to lift her up in front of the kids, to show appropriate affection for her, and to model the respect for her that you want your girls to have. Lila can be your best ally in this effort if she is reassured of your devotion with quality love.

Pennsylvania-licensed psychologist Georgia Shaffer adds,

Dennis must not forget what his relationship with Lila is modeling for his daughters. No matter what his words say, his daughters may be learning from his actions that children are more important than our spouse. Is this the message he wants to communicate?

Chuck notes that the dynamic at play here is the fact that showing respect for Lila is the best thing Dennis can do to give his daughters a strong self-esteem. It is a win-win. Dennis has stated that his daughters are the most important. The best thing he can do for them is to give them a model that they will internalize: a good husband puts his wife first. The daughters win. Lila wins. Victoria Jackson, LCSW, agrees:

The girls will respect the fact that their parents value the spousal relationship enough to set boundaries and spend special time together.

By observing this behavior, Dennis's girls will re-create it in their own marriages; they will select husbands who put them first. If one of them dates someone who does not show her respect, she will quit going out with the guy because Dennis's behavior will have taught her what to expect. I think all parents want their child to select a mate who values and respects her. By respecting Lila, Dennis has the opportunity to positively influence his daughters' future happiness.

Additionally, showing disrespect for any woman is bad for his daughters. Demanding that his daughters respect both their mother and stepmother will ultimately be good for their self-esteem. Dennis may think that by putting his girls above Lila he is helping them feel good about themselves and feel important and special to him. However, the best way for him to do this is to build up women in general and then to invest in the girls' lives by going to their games, recitals, and spending time with them—but not by putting them above their stepmother and entering her into a power struggle.

Susan Rogers makes the following suggestions for Dennis to help him model respect for Lila:

Small blessings, like noticing what is needed and taking care of it without being asked or reminded by her, will go a long way in helping her to feel treasured. When she stresses, just listen. Ask God, "What is she feeling or thinking?" and then share with her what you have heard. A little empathy will push the "Ah-ha, he loves me" button. Anxiety goes down, and everyone can relax. The worst thing you can do is to get defensive, so avoid it—though this is where most men fail. Truly, her anxious words do not pose a threat to you, unless you allow them to do so.

Dennis should also look at his own insecurities. Gaylen Larson talked about a man's need for significance and importance. By putting the girls first, Dennis could be meeting his own need for importance, drawing them to himself rather than to him and Lila together. In addressing Lila's situation, Rose Sweet says,

> More often than not, it is the new husband who dishes out the rejection and serves it up with a generous dollop of false guilt, hoping to get the focus off himself.

She advises Dennis and Lila to take a few sessions together—alone and uninterrupted:

> Share, talk, and explore, but do not just dump emotions on each other. Be clear about identifying your fears, needs, and possible solutions. Lila needs to make a list of specific emotional, physical, and financial needs and give examples of how she would like those met. When sharing her needs with Dennis, she should be open to, and ask him to come up with, his own style, choice, or options in meeting those needs so he does not feel too controlled.

If after several clear discussions about how to change the dynamics, Dennis and Lila cannot come to an agreement, it is probably time to reeducate themselves on the basics: what God expects from husbands/wives regarding their spouses' needs. He says a man is to love his wife in the same way Jesus loves the church—to love so extravagantly that he would lay down his life for her (Ephesians 5:25). He does not say the same to the man in his role as a father. While it is assumed that most fathers love their children, they are not instructed by God to love their children in the same way they are asked to love their spouse. Instead, they are first commanded to teach, guide, and train the children (Deuteronomy 6:7). As simple and as exaggerated as it sounds, a man should train his children in love, but be willing to die for his wife (if that's what it takes!)—the true definition of loving extravagantly.

God's order for the family says that Dennis and Lila are one flesh. That relationship comes before the children. By putting Lila ahead of his daughters when they are in her home, Dennis is modeling godly order and is letting the girls know that they cannot rule over their stepmother.

ANOTHER MOTHER

Dennis' daughters will always be a part of his life, as they should be. Beyond simply accepting that fact, the difficulty for Lila comes in figuring out what her role in their lives should be. Her resentful attitude is pushing them away. Lila may be feeling the same things Sherrie felt in adjusting to her stepchildren and their presence in her life.

> I saw the resentment in their eyes and despised myself for being unable (or unwilling) to manage the awful feelings that percolated within me.

Rather than pushing the girls away, Lila needs to develop a relationship with them. Susan Rogers says,

> Yes, they will resist you, but in time they will appreciate the grace you extended to them during this difficult time. Blended families are by nature birthed in loss. The children enter the new family setting with fragile emotions and insecurities. They are not equipped to handle the losses and changes of the adult world. Yet they are expected to adapt, to hide their fears, and to pretend that this unnatural situation is A-okay. They are torn between their love for their father with a strong desire to please him and loyalty to their mother with a strong desire to keep the peace.

Georgia Shaffer encourages Lila to establish a relationship with her two stepdaughters:

> Start by finding one activity the three of you enjoy. It may be shopping, cooking, making candles, or going to the hair stylist. By focusing on that special activity, the conversation will begin to flow and the relationships gradually will be established.

Along those same lines, Sherrie shares what happened when she was willing to put herself in the children's shoes:

> I realized that no matter how much attention Bob gave them during the weekend visits, it could never make up for what was taken from them. They were innocently caught in the middle.

From her own experience, Kathy agrees:

Whatever the circumstances were for their parents' divorce, children feel that they have lost the non-custodial parent. They may have some fears, real or imagined, just as Lila does.

To help the girls deal with their own fears and insecurities, Susan Rogers suggests,

Try to create an environment for the girls where they feel at home and not like visitors. Let them have their own furniture, hair products, clothing, and other personal items in their own room, as well as a love note to await them each weekend. Hauling stuff back and forth just increases the feeling that this is not really their home, rather only a place to visit. All females need to feel they have a "spot," and they will be restless and insecure until they know deep within their hearts that this is their home too. So make every effort and give it some time.

To help the girls deal with the loss and role confusion, Lila needs to develop an appropriate relationship with them. But what should that relationship be? Susan Rogers says,

Put your efforts into being a good friend rather than focusing so much on being a good parent. Children of divorce need your special friendship, Lila, not your competition.

Adjusting to the new role is often difficult, as stepchildren have another mother. Stephanie reflects on her experience by saying,

I cannot take her place or take claim to anything she has done in the past.

Then what can the stepmother do? Sherrie found this approach worked very well for her:

This may sound strange, but to keep myself from taking on an all or nothing attitude, I began to think of myself as the kids' aunt or Sunday school teacher. They didn't need or want another mother, but it wasn't unreasonable to expect that we could have a mutually respectful relationship. I leave all the instruction, correction, and guidance to Bob—I take on a supportive role. Before each visit I ask Bob what he has in mind for the weekend so I know what to expect.

I began to view the weekends as the "guys' time." This was a choice that helped me lose those ugly feelings of jealousy and competition. It also gave me permission to work on my own interactions or visit a friend—plans to look forward to. To keep continuity, we always have meals together and share at least one activity as a family unit.

Within Sherrie's comments are many valuable tips that she learned the hard way. Sherrie's concept of viewing herself as a Sunday school teacher or aunt is a great way to deal with the relationship, providing care while allowing room for growth. Many stepmothers try too hard to make the new family into their perception of the perfect "Brady Bunch" household.

While writing this chapter I went to lunch with some friends. When I brought up the topic, one friend affirmed that she had tried too hard in the beginning. She tried to force the blended family, made up of adolescents, to take outings and vacations together, with dismal results. Upon hearing this, one of the other women at the table exclaimed, "Kids at that age don't want to be with their parents anyway, stepparent or otherwise!" So true, and in hindsight it seemed so obvious. But in her effort to do everything right, my friend tried too hard to make it all work. Sensing her frustration, her husband told her to relax, to not try so hard. She heeded his advice and has found things have gone much more smoothly.

Jean Cox-Turner affirms the idea that older kids don't want to be with their parents:

> Teenagers go through a stage of wanting acceptance and belonging. What their peers think about them means everything. With this in mind, a lot of teens become rebellious, especially toward their parents.

Susan Rogers agrees:

> Trying to blend two families is no small task; however, God has more than enough love to spread through each of you for the members of the merging family. Remember, it takes one year for each year of the child's life to accept you as a parent figure. So you might as well just relax and be a friend. Therefore, it is unrealistic to expect a traditional two-parent family environment. The trick is to flex, connect with other adults who have walked this road, read more on blended families, and pray for greater love.

Extravagant love!

Through this book, we hope to help parents like Lila connect with other adults who have walked this road. By seeing what others have been through, you know you are not in this boat alone. Sherrie now says,

> I look forward to the visits. Interestingly, the boys are now eager to share themselves with me and seek my participation. My tank is filled by the joy I see in my husband's face as he freely enjoys his few days a month with his children. I am encouraged as well because I know the boys will be healthier adults as a result of the changes we've made.

It seems like the topsy-turvy days of visitation awkwardness will never end, but they can smooth out and become enjoyable for everyone.

The Interaction

FOR THE MOTHER:

1. Create a list with complete descriptions of what behaviors your husband should display in front of the girls that will make you feel like you are number one. For example: open the car door for you; seat you at the table.

2. Build up the self-esteem of the girls by engaging them in age-appropriate activities that they enjoy. For example: take teens shopping for clothes or makeup if that is their focus; attend their athletic events if they are involved in sports.

FOR THE FATHER:

1. Use your treatment of your wife as a means of modeling how a husband treats his wife.

2. Create a list with complete descriptions of what behaviors you will display in front of the girls that will make you feel like your wife feels that she is number one. For example: (Wrong) Father: "Lila, would you do the dishes so the girls and I can go to the movies?" (Right): Father: "Okay, girls, I want you to clear the table and wash the dishes. When you're done, Lila will take you to the mall.

5

PERSONAL
ISSUES

Chapter FOURTEEN

Married From Our Dysfunctions

Maturity, Respect, and Honor

The Issue

*E*d and Elizabeth have been married for fourteen years. They married when they were both brand-new Christians. Ed was barely divorced from his first wife at the time. They married more from their mutual dysfunctions and neediness rather than from a whole heart desiring to give and to love each other. After all these years both of them have been through many changes. Elizabeth, a Popular Sanguine/Powerful Choleric, has spent a great deal of time with God, counselors, and self-help books and sees herself as an entirely different person. She feels she can now relate to and experience a much healthier relationship. However, from Elizabeth's point of view, Ed, a Perfect Melancholy, has not grown as she has. She believes she has overcome so many things only to find that her husband has not come with her, nor does he want to. Ed and Elizabeth are currently seeing a counselor and considering divorce.

Insights

Given what we know about Elizabeth and Ed, two key issues can make an almost instant difference in this troubled relationship: first, maturity, and then respect and honor. Since we have limited facts in this case, we have addressed the subject with a broad brush in hopes of touching not only Ed and Elizabeth's situation, but circumstances in your life as well.

MATURITY

Since Elizabeth says that she has grown both as a person and as a Christian, let's accept that she is the more mature. Chuck advises, however, that if she has grown out of her marriage, maybe she hasn't really grown at all. As a Christian, Elizabeth needs to look at the overall teaching of God's Word. Throughout the Bible she will find many verses that point to God's belief in marriage and its priority. For example, Matthew 19:4–6 says,

> "Haven't you read," [Jesus] replied, "that at the beginning the Creator 'made them male and female,' and said, 'For this reason a man will leave his father and mother and be united to his wife, and the two will become one flesh'? So they are no longer two, but one. Therefore what God has joined together, let man not separate" (NIV).

Remember, God never advises us to do something that is contrary to the overall teachings in his Word. If a person's growth has caused that person to be unhappy with his/her spouse, is that what God wants?

Elizabeth's story hit home for Lindsay as she too seeks growth at a different pace than her husband. This is her second marriage, and like Elizabeth and Ed, was near divorce. Lindsay suggests that Elizabeth look at what she has learned from all those self-help books.

> Is there anything you have learned that is contrary to the Word of God? Does God want to tear up marriages or strengthen them? What lies are you listening to, nourishing, or heeding that you would consider divorce?

Melanie Wilson, Ph.D., warns Elizabeth about becoming dependent on the self-help books as they can easily become a false god, "a lover that can cause jealousy for God—and Elizabeth's husband." Additionally, Chuck often advises people to throw away their self-help books that focus on "self." The biblical mandate is not to watch out for self but to display Christlike love—extravagant love—toward others. He suggests that if a book or an activity doesn't draw us closer to God and closer to our spouse, it is doing more harm than good. Use that as a yardstick to measure marital satisfaction.

I am a great fan of Gary Thomas' work, especially his book *Sacred Marriage*. I suggest that Elizabeth read it carefully. In it, Gary says,

> It is not the better part of godliness to let one's spiritual duties eclipse one's marital responsibilities. What most divorces mean is that at least one party, and possibly both, have ceased to put the gospel first in their lives. They no longer live by Paul's guiding principle, "I make it my goal to please Him," because the Bible makes it clear in its teaching. God says, "I hate divorce" (Malachi 2:16). If the goal of the couple was to please God, they wouldn't seek divorce.[1]

Melanie Wilson adds,

> Christian women often pursue a spiritual journey without including their husbands. I always recommend that couples communicate what they're learning and why they're excited without the expectation that the spouse will follow the same path. We can easily use our growth as a way of one-upping our spouse. When I became very excited about daily prayer and Bible study through Becky Tirabassi's materials, I could tell that my husband felt left out. I bought him his own Bible and prayer journal and he feels more included—even though he does not use them the way I do.

Gaylen Larson, Ph.D., encourages Elizabeth to include her husband in her growth process as Melanie has included hers:

> It's important for Elizabeth to look at how she might be pushing Ed away by her self-help growth. He will not want to discuss subjects that make him feel "less-than." If she can structure the discussion about a book as asking for his advice, or hold the discussion in such a way that his opinion is held in high regard, it will no longer be a threat. She may find him unconsciously wanting to be more involved.

If Ed does becomes interested in joining Elizabeth, Michelle Holman, MA, LPC, offers this advice:

> One tool I've found very useful for couples in this situation is for them to make a commitment to read together Fred and Florence Littauer's book *Daily Marriage Builders for Couples* at least three times a week. I have seen several couples who've done this grow closer to God and to each other. They become more accepting of each other's personalities and the gifts each brings with it.

Lindsay advises Elizabeth to write on the tablet of her heart one hundred times a day,

Divorce is not an option. Divorce is not an option. Or make it more of a positive affirmation: *By my submitting to God, our marriage is a source of comfort and joy* or *In marriage, my husband and I not only survive, but thrive.*

This is one of the techniques Lindsay has used successfully to help her reframe her own situation.

Once we accept the concept that divorce is not an option, and acknowledge that Elizabeth is the more mature, we see that she holds the responsibility to love Ed unconditionally with the Lord's love. Again we look to God's Word for guidance. Repeatedly the Bible admonishes us to love one another as Christ loved us— especially the unlovable. In a difficult marriage, the unlovable is often the spouse. If one spouse claims to be the stronger Christian, she/he holds the greater responsibility to display that love; what I like to call loving extravagantly, based on Ephesians 5:1–2 from *The Message*:

> Observe how Christ loved us. His love is not cautious but extravagant. He didn't love in order to get something from us but to give everything of himself to us; love like that.

Elizabeth needs to love her husband as he is, not expecting anything in return— not to get, but to give. When she does this, she will find that her husband is apt to be more responsive to growth himself.

RESPECT AND HONOR

This brings us to the idea of respect and honor. Sylvia offers,

> My husband of thirty-nine years is also a Perfect Melancholy. Like Elizabeth, I am Popular Sanguine/Powerful Choleric. Through the years, I have learned several things. I've learned that my husband thrives on admiration and respect. If he senses he is not meeting my expectations, he withdraws. My expectations make him feel judged and cause an atmosphere that is not loving, creating a worsening cycle. Jesus tells me that my job is loving, not judging.

In their book *Intimate Allies*, Dan Allender and Tremper Longman III spotlight this concept:

> Marriage requires a radical commitment to love our spouses as they are, while longing for them to be what they are not yet. Every marriage moves either toward enhancing one another's glory or toward degrading each other.[2]

Lindsay encourages Elizabeth to pray for a "spiritual mother," a mature older woman with a solid marriage whom she can go to for help. Lindsay says,

> Once when I was irritated at my husband, I asked my spiritual mother what she did when she wanted to "pop her husband in the chops." She laughed and told me to pray and ask God to give me his love for my husband when I don't have any love of my own.

Lindsay knows from experience that God is faithful to answer this prayer!

Another aspect of this situation is the couple's personalities. Again, Elizabeth needs to take the lead. By nature, the Popular Sanguine is the most inclined to change. The Popular Sanguine wants everyone to be happy. She can make adjustments in herself if it will make the other person happy. I claim Romans 12:18 here: "If possible, so far as it depends on you, be at peace with all men." (NASB) I believe that God added the disclaimer because it is impossible to be at peace with all men. After all, we can only control our own behaviors—but we can't control them! The verse puts the responsibility for peace in the relationship on ourselves, not expecting the other person to change. Sylvia says,

> My husband is only going to read *Consumer's Report*, the *Wall Street Journal*, and our local newspaper. I am an avid reader and self-improver. I can make any changes I want in my own behavior, but have only the power to make my own decisions and choices.

Lindsay suggests that Elizabeth stop "fiddling" with trying to force changes on her husband and then leave the changing to the Holy Spirit. She says,

> I have this image of my husband and the Holy Spirit on a football field. The Holy Spirit does not need me down on my husband's playing field, but in his grandstand. I hope I have the grace to cheer him on instead of booing him. I think it is deplorable when fans boo the home team!

Chuck agrees with Lindsay's concept. He sees the need for Elizabeth to offer more encouragement and support to Ed, to compliment him frequently. His counsel to Elizabeth is to identify the strengths of the marriage. One strength is that the marriage has provided her with an environment conducive to personal growth. Perhaps she has overlooked that and attributes all of her growth to the self-help books.

Michelle Holman says,

I would also encourage Elizabeth to begin creating a "gratitude list" in a journal. Each day list at least three of Ed's qualities or actions that she observed for which she was grateful. As she begins to embrace an attitude of gratitude toward Ed, I suggest that she share these with him.

Sylvia talks about her own marriage:

Sometimes we can focus on the negatives rather than the positives. When a negative about him begins to obsess my mind, I find stopping and making a list of all his wonderful attributes helps give me a better perspective. "I" statements spoken in truth and love help release hurt feelings. I try to stay away from the "you" or "if you would only" statements, which seem like a put-down.

While it is much easier to say than actually do, Elizabeth needs to lovingly submit to Ed, not because he deserves it, but because she is really submitting to the Lord when she honors and respects her husband.

What about you? Whether you are the husband or the wife, are there factors in common with Ed and Elizabeth's marriage and yours? What can you learn from their situation?

The Interaction

FOR THE WIFE:

1. Describe specifically how things would be different if your husband were the spiritual heavyweight in the home. The greater the detail the better.

2. List what you are doing to bring about your half of the ideal home that you envision.

3. List specifically what you expect from your husband in achieving this goal. How would your husband be different if he were the spiritual leader of the home? Have you given him permission and the opportunity to be the spiritual leader or has he been in a one-down position where he feels that he cannot compete?

4. What role has your spouse played in the current level of growth that you now enjoy?

FOR THE HUSBAND:

1. Describe the changes you have seen in your wife over the years and how you feel about them.

2. What steps are you willing to take to fulfill the role as spiritual leader in your home?

Weepy Most of the Time
Depression

The Issue

Sarah is a wife, a mother of two, and a Christian. She and her husband, Stewart, have a happy marriage, she has a fulfilling job, is active in ministry, and spends quality time with her family. Looking at her life, everything appears to be in order. However, for the last year Sarah has discovered that her energy is low, she has trouble concentrating at work, and she feels weepy most of the time.

Sarah's paternal grandfather was depressed (according to family members) but was undiagnosed medically. Her sister, who is not a Christian, has been medicated for depression for several years and is doing well. Sarah's physician checked her for low thyroid and other ailments without finding any physical cause for her symptoms. He believes that she is depressed and would like to start her on antidepressants.

At the encouragement of well-meaning friends, Sarah has searched her heart for unresolved sin issues. The women in her small group have advised her to find her joy in the Lord, increase her daily prayer time, and wait it out. Stewart thinks this is a spiritual issue and that if she really was a good Christian she would be able to "snap out of it." Over time, Sarah's depression has turned into a major stress on their marriage. She feels she has tried everything and is in need of help.

Insights

As the symptoms described in Sarah's situation have gained awareness in the medical community as depression, it has created a conflict within the Christian community. Is this a spiritual issue? Is it a medical issue? Where do we draw the lines? While there is no way this brief chapter will resolve this controversy once and for all, we do hope to shed some light on the subject by sharing what others have done in similar situations and to offer the advice—though sometimes conflicting—of professionals. The difference of opinion represented here reflects the ongoing debate.

If you, or your spouse, struggle with depression, we encourage you to prayerfully read through the following pages to help determine which course of action is the best for you. Solutions for depression tend to fall into two camps. We are calling one "Nourish your soul" and the other "Take your pills." Both have proven to be effective for different people.

We believe that any time a condition, such as depression, is threatening the foundation of an otherwise solid marriage, loving extravagantly may mean setting aside your own beliefs on the issue and doing what it takes to help your spouse—not to get, but to give.

NOURISH YOUR SOUL

Some people believe that depression is always a spiritual issue and should be handled with a strictly spiritual cure. While there may be sin issues that need to be addressed, and dealing with them may help, simply telling someone to "get right with the Lord" usually does more harm than good. In talking about her own depression, Barb said,

> I didn't want the ladies in my Bible study to know. I was scared they would think I was a sham.

Robin agrees:

> I have been in Sarah's shoes and found the Christian community eager to "shoot the wounded" with arrows of false guilt, ignorance, and fear—even pastors. One of the most urgent needs in the church today is simple, solid teaching that depression is a real medical illness and that medicine and psychotherapy are legitimate tools that God can use.

Chuck worked with a seventeen-year-old girl who was depressed. She had been to four different pastors who told her that it was all in her head and that she needed to get right with God. The guilt and hopelessness created by their well-meaning counsel resulted in an attempted suicide. As Chuck worked with her, it was discovered that she had adult ADHD and was put on medication. She went from being suicidal to graduating from college, getting married, and going on to lead a normal life.

If a person like Sarah has searched his or her life for potential "sin issues" or other causes and not found any unresolved concerns—yet the depression remains—there are still many non-medical options available. All of us need an element of them in our lives—whether or not we are facing depression.

As Barb did, you might want to try these before going the medical route, or in conjunction with it. After reading Sarah's story, Barb wrote,

> I have been there. On the outside I was the motivator and the upbeat person in every group in which I was involved. When I came home, I started falling apart. I often felt like crying and only got out of bed because I knew my children needed me. My kindergartner was always late to school because I couldn't find the keys to drive the car. My doctor suggested I might be experiencing depression.

Barb's doctor recommended that she get some exercise daily, like taking a walk. He also advised her to cut back on any non-required responsibilities and find a hobby or interest she could get passionate about. Today Barb reports,

> It's working! I walk, garden (the fresh air certainly helps), and paint. My husband noticed I am smiling more and playing with the kids and him more. I think many women tend to overextend themselves and not even realize it—whether they are working moms or stay at home. Stay-at-home moms feel they need to prove they did something all day and working moms feel they need to make up for the time they spend at work. The result is we are all stressed out. God doesn't expect us to do it all, and he doesn't need us to do it all! He just wants us to love and worship him. Once I cleared away the unnecessary noise in my life, I could enjoy God's gifts.

Chuck adds,

> Depression is one of the Enemy's best tools to distance people from God. He loves it when people do not get help.

Sylvia is a nurse, married thirty-nine years, and a mother of six children. She has battled depression for twenty years. From her personal and professional experience, she adds,

> Depression is often a battle of the mind that Satan uses to condemn us and to plant worrisome, anxious, and negative thoughts. We must equip ourselves and renew our mind as Ephesians 4:22–24 instructs; we cannot wallow in negative

thoughts. Police your thoughts and when negative ones begin, take the sword of the Spirit and fill your mind with the Word of God (Ephesians 6:13, 17). Meditate on verses like Joshua 1:9, "I command you—be strong and courageous! Do not be afraid or discouraged. For the LORD your God is with you wherever you go" (NLT). As a depressed person, it is sometimes hard to get the fuzz out of your mind to concentrate. Sometimes taking a simple verse such as Psalm 23:1 and saying it over and over [with different emphases] helps:

The LORD is my shepherd.
The Lord IS my shepherd.
The Lord is MY shepherd.
The Lord is my SHEPHERD.

Remember the instruction in Philippians 4:8 to fill your mind with everything that is beautiful. There is a battleground in the mind, and we must become good warriors and learn to fight. Don't let negative, depressing thoughts consume you.

Sylvia encourages Sarah by saying that she is doing many things right. Since we are created with a spirit, mind, and body, we need to take care of all three. Sylvia admonishes Sarah to look at all the options. She says,

The medical community wants to throw medicine at anyone with depression, but there are other ways. Some studies show that depressed people usually have low serotonin or dopamine levels. Exercise increases the levels of these good chemicals. I recommend adding something in your life in the way of exercise: water aerobics, tennis, golf, walking the dog, swimming. Put something creative in your life: take watercolor classes, decorate birdhouses, plant a garden. The act of creating causes good things to happen. Filling your mind with the beautiful and powerful words of God's love in Scripture is good—or reading a lovely devotional book. Laughter is helpful. Singing increases good chemicals—even in the shower. But stress increases bad ones.

Like Sarah, Chuck has a family history of depression, and he has battled it most of his life. He has found that exercise makes a major difference. He likes to mountain bike. I prefer inline skating. When I am out of town he usually rides his bike, and when I am in town we make a major effort to skate together, often spending three hours at a stretch in physical activity—even in the dead of winter! While I do not have a constant struggle with the "black dog," as Winston Churchill called it, I find that exercise is important for me too. It is one of the ways I "nourish my soul."

Chuck and I have also found that his eating habits drastically affect his moods. If he eats well and regularly, his mood is more stable. If I sense he is getting irritable and grumpy, I'll ask, "When was the last time you ate?" He has learned this coded communication and asks, "Am I grumpy?" For my own sanity, I try to keep some protein with me when we travel, and he has learned to take responsibility for eating what he has learned his body needs. Even while I am at home writing, I have dinner in the Crockpot waiting for him the moment he walks in the door. This is one way I can love him extravagantly.

Sylvia agrees and advises Sarah to check her nutrition:

> Is she skipping breakfast or lunch? Is she low on iron, vitamins A or K, calcium, or magnesium? Depression can be caused by poor nutrition.

Anne says that, like Sarah, she had all the earmarks of success. Yet through counseling she learned that she had very helpless, unproductive ways of handling life situations. Anne says,

> I changed the way I think and interact with myself, my husband, my children, my clients, my colleagues—even the guy in the fruit and vegetable department at the grocery store.

Following up on Anne's comment, Sylvia encourages Sarah to look at her life:

> Do you need a different kind of life? A new job? Are you overwhelmed with work and family? Do you have relationships that are upsetting you? Do you feel loved and valued? Do you have a heart friend—one to whom you can tell it like it is?

Sometimes making changes in the things that we can change make a big difference. Other times we can clearly see the stressors that are causing the depression yet are unable to do anything about it. I've mentioned a tough time in Chuck's and my life. For five months economic forces caused Chuck to live in Colorado while they forced me to stay in New Mexico. They were very difficult months—as were the months immediately before and after. During that time I cried at the drop of a hat. I felt like I was on the verge of tears all the time. I cried out to God and I often cried myself to sleep, alone in our big bed—except for my fluffy schnauzer, Tucker, whom I made sleep next to me even though he prefers the floor. I knew the exact cause of my depression, and I could see that Chuck and I were making the best of a very difficult situation. But that did not mean that I liked it! I started taking Saint-John's-wort and found that it helped stabilize my moods and helped get me through that difficult time.

Sylvia suggests that if Sarah has tried these "nourish your soul" approaches and they have not made a noticeable positive change, that she then look at taking something natural, like Saint-John's-wort or SAMe (S-Adenosyl-Methionine). These "natural" remedies are controversial, but many people have found them helpful. If you struggle with depression, you might want to do some additional research on the herbal alternatives. If your study indicates that they may be helpful in your situation, try them. Additionally, Mike Sievert, M.D., advises that even with the natural treatments, you should be under the care of a doctor who is familiar with them.

TAKE YOUR PILLS

Sarah's doctor wants to put her on antidepressants. As we have said, Sarah's sister has been taking them successfully for several years. Sarah's grandfather also struggled with depression, though in his time depression was not labeled as a medical condition. These factors combine to indicate that Sarah's condition—which contains all the symptoms of classic depression—is more than a spiritual issue. Gaylen Larson, Ph.D., says of Sarah's case,

> She may have a biochemical imbalance as well as a heredity precondition. We know that depression runs in families, just like diabetes. If you are trying to deal with the symptoms instead of the cause, you will never have true victory.

If the depression is truly a chemical imbalance and a hereditary issue, some form of medication may be needed. It should be looked at not as something that will cure the condition, but rather to keep it in check—like insulin works for a diabetic. Neither Sarah nor her husband should expect the medication for depression to be a short-term remedy. Anti-depressants are not addictive. Studies of long-term use (ten years) show no adverse affects.

There does seem to be a long-term benefit of medication. The brain appears to "rewire" itself even after the medication is discontinued. Like any medicine, antidepressants must be used with the careful supervision of an experienced psychiatrist. (Women should see a psychiatrist who understands menopausal/hormonal fluctuations and their impact on depression.)

Based on experience with two friends with chemical imbalances, Bev says,

> If it is clinical depression, she will probably need to be on medication for at least three years. So many people think they are fine, quit taking the medications, and fall back to where they were—or farther—due to their disappointment that they were not healed.

If Sarah's doctor has checked hormones and chemical balances like thyroid function, and they are all OK, Sarah needs to listen to her doctor and take the recommended medications. If her husband hesitates, have the doctor or some other trusted individual like their pastor (if he is in agreement) talk frankly with her husband. She needs to get medical attention before she hits bottom, is hospitalized, and has the stigma of mental illness added to her concerns. Depression can be hereditary, but siblings may not show symptoms at the same age. Spiritual and marital problems come because of the response of others and their attitude toward this kind of chemical imbalance.

The longer depression goes without treatment, the harder it is to reverse—even to the point that it becomes irreversible. Many irreversible cases end in suicide.

While our focus is on Sarah, depression affects men and women alike. Doreen had an experience with her husband, Woody, and his chemical imbalance. They met at a Christian college and married some time later. They seemed well and happy to everyone around them. However, a few years into the marriage depression set in and accelerated to the point that Woody could no longer go to work. He was diagnosed as manic-depressive (which is now called bipolar). When he stayed on his medication, he functioned. When he didn't, he did not function. No matter how rational or irrational his behavior was, a well-meaning Christian counselor advised Doreen to submit to her husband despite the physical abuse that often accompanied his mood swings. "It is your wifely duty," she said. Finally, after many years, Doreen left in hopes of having a semblance of a normal life. Yet many people in her church thought Doreen broke up an ideal Christian marriage. What the church friends saw was the outer shell of chaos. All three of their adult children are finding they have inherited the condition from their father and are experiencing some of his symptoms. They have learned from his example and vow to take their medication regularly.

In discussing bipolar disorder, Gaylen Larson adds,

> Many people with bipolar are misdiagnosed because they only seek help when they are depressed. Treating the depression is only part of the problem, as antidepressants are not really what is needed.

A pastor's wife I met at a conference told me that her husband had been opposed to medication for depression until she had a bout with it that virtually incapacitated her. She was placed on medication for long enough to lift her out of the darkness. She did not have the family history or the other symptoms that would indicate a long need for medication.

Chuck says that for some people depression comes upon them due to circumstances, medical reasons, or a combination of both. Once they are in the pit of depression, life looks so bleak that they cannot see their way through to the light at the end of the tunnel. In these cases, medication is helpful to lift them up enough that they can deal with their situation in a logical and rational manner. Once the situation has been addressed and dealt with, the medication is no longer needed. Such was the case with this pastor's wife. Her husband is now a believer that sometimes medication is the best option.

Ann told us the following story:

When I was forty-two, I was so depressed that I was considering bloodless ways to commit suicide. (I didn't want to leave any ugly stains.) Finally I sought help. I started interviewing counselors, and it took each of them about thirty-two seconds to diagnose me as clinically depressed—even though logically I could tell myself that my life was great. The medication prescribed by my psychiatrist began to remove the bleakness in about twenty to thirty days. It took nine months before I did not need it anymore. Through the combination of medication and counseling, I learned to change my destructive behavior patterns.

Eight years later I am happier than I have ever been in my life—even though my husband's company was downsized and he took early retirement, we're facing an empty nest, my mom's health is declining, and I'm starting a new career as primary breadwinner (all significant life changes). No matter how much I prayed, I doubt I would have had the insights I gained through counseling. Just being faithful does not insulate us from depression, illness, poor judgment, or misfortune.

Bev said about her friend,

How wonderful that today we know she has a chemical problem. Sarah should not fiddle around with this. It actually can be life-threatening if it escalates into certain types of problems. She has evidence of depression, but she does not know what chemical imbalance is feeding it or what may develop from this point. Catching it close to the beginning of the slide is more effective than waiting to see if it becomes a full-blown illness. Yes, God can heal her. If he does, the medications will not hurt her, and her response can be seen as evidence of less or no need for them. In the meantime, take action.

Depression is a real issue. While both Chuck and I have had periods of depression with different probable causes and different approaches to treatment, I was surprised at the volume of response and the degree of passion I received when I posted Sarah's scenario. This is a real problem for many people today, even those in strong Christian marriages.

If depression is a factor in your marriage, do not let it ruin your relationship. You might try the non-medical solutions first—after all, exercise and activities that stimulate us are good for everyone, depressed or not. If the medical answer turns out to be the right one for you, the non-medical activities can only increase the medication's effectiveness. However, Mike Sievert advises,

> Do not mix the herbal remedies with the conventional antidepressants, and be sure to be under supervision of a psychiatrist who is familiar with the treatment of depression and its possible side effects.

Gaylen Larson adds,

> I have seen marriage problems disappear when the depression gets under control through the use of medication.

Whichever approach works for you, follow Bev's advice and take your depression seriously.

The Interaction

1. Both parties will agree to mutually submit as delineated in Ephesians.

2. The husband will submit to the wife by agreeing to meet together with a Christian psychiatrist. The husband should go prepared with questions addressing his concerns and objections.

3. The husband is to take the initiative to learn about depression so his comments are educated. He might achieve this by going to the local medical library—perhaps at a university—or searching the Internet with the goal of finding documented, scientific research on both sides of the depression debate. ("Documented, scientific" is suggested because the Internet is full of odd sites.)

4. The wife will submit to the husband's perspective by continuing to pursue all avenues of a spiritual solution. Additionally, the wife will commit to a healthy diet and regular exercise.

5. The wife will go to the family doctor to rule out any other medical causes such as menopausal/hormonal fluctuations or thyroid dysfunction.

6. As all of the solutions proposed within the chapter are good options, the couple will commit to pursuing all options without bias. Many people feel torn within the power struggle of which model is better, which only exacerbates the issue.

Meeting Others' Expectations

Childlessness, Outside Pressures, Full Life

The Issue

"Yes, I will marry you, but there will be no children." Dena can still remember saying those words many years ago. Brad, her husband-to-be, was more than willing to agree to the "no children" clause. Both had been extremely hurt in their first marriages and had built major walls to protect themselves from any further pain.

The years rolled on. They had a good marriage, not a great one, but still better than some. They loved each other. Seven years into the marriage Dena reached thirty. She began asking herself the very difficult question, "Do I want to remain childless for the rest of my life?" On one hand, they had become very selfish with their time and money and having a baby would really upset the apple cart. On the other hand, they were the only couple in both families to remain childless. Dena was not pressuring herself, but was feeling pressure from family members, friends, people with whom she worked, even members of their church. It is amazing how cruel some people can be when you do not meet their expectations of how you should live your life.

While Brad and Dena are happy with their place in life and their decision, the pressure put on them by other well-meaning people has made Dena question her life. For six months she has had trouble sleeping, roaming the house at night with her mind playing the same old tune over and over again: "You are such a disappointment to everyone."

Both Brad and Dena have good jobs they enjoy. However, they feel they are missing something.

Insights

While it may seem that this situation applies to very few, the responses we received indicate that it is indeed a problem in need of a prescription. Laura wrote,

> I know making a choice to not have children isn't a popular opinion, and I certainly don't expect many others to share it. Occasionally I run across a woman who is brave enough to express the same emotions. We connect instantly because most people think we are weird. I am responding because I've rarely seen anyone brave enough to address this topic.

Laura's words ring true for many couples, including us. Whether "brave" or foolish, if you are willing to say, "I made this choice and I am okay with it," the response is emphatic. Almost every childless couple has felt, at some time or another, shunned or misplaced by their status.

In discussing her childless status, Melody says,

> I have felt like an outsider in society. I used to dread meeting new people who would invariably ask if we had children. In shaking my head, I felt like I was confessing to a crime or admitting I had a terrible deformity.

Some of those who offered their stories are like Laura, Dena, and myself. We either knew all along that we did not want children, or our biological clocks ran out and we never had any. Others, like Melody and her husband, Pride, and JoAnn and her husband, Brian, wanted children only to find that they were unable to conceive. JoAnn reported,

> We have experienced society's condemning looks when we have told them we do not have children, especially when we have not explained why. We stopped explaining because it was actually easier to receive "the look" that condemned us as selfish than it was to explain everything we had gone through and have people say, "Don't worry, it will happen."

When Amanda and Tony got married, they decided not to have children. Then after a few years of marriage they decided they did want children, but "try as we might, it didn't happen." Of the pressure of meeting other's expectations, she says,

> No one has given me a hard time about not having children because I have found it easier to say, "We tried and it didn't work." I have a sense that if I hadn't used that line, people would have pushed harder.

In a magazine article entitled "Married Without Children: A Curse or a Call?" Jan Coleman writes,

> A couple in their early forties was constantly asked, "What if everybody decided not to have children?" The wife stated, "It bewilders most people and makes them uneasy. Somehow, they think we selfishly opted for fun and freedom over the love of a child. Rarely does anyone understand."[1]

Whew! It is not just me who has felt the pressure. I remember visiting with a noted Christian author. When the conversation came to the inevitable subject of children and he found out that I did not have any, he vowed to pray for me, stating, "Everyone I pray for gets pregnant!" "Don't you dare," I ventured. Yes, my mother is disappointed that there are no "little Maritas." She finally quit asking about children when I quipped, "I will have them when you stay home and take care of them." Or perhaps it's because Chuck and I have been married for eighteen years without children that she has given up.

The pressure Dena feels is real. First, we'll look at dealing with the pressures and expectations of others, and then at living a full and happy life without children. Whether your situation matches Brad and Dena's—or like Melody, JoAnn, and Amanda, you wanted children but never had them—you will find help on the following pages.

OUTSIDE PRESSURES

When we operate outside of what the rest of the world considers the norm, we will always have questions, or at least "the look," as JoAnn describes it. Melody addresses others' expectations.

> Like any lifestyle choice—especially one outside of the standard routine—not everyone will understand. For instance, several missionary friends of mine tell me their families reject the choice they have made to serve the Lord in a foreign country for little pay. They must constantly protect the choice they have made from criticism by others. However, they are able to do this because they have a firm commitment to their choice, they have a sense of inner peace about it, and they believe it is their appointed path from God. Remaining childless is a very

valid choice that can be freeing and rewarding in many ways. However, because it is not the usual choice people make, couples need to feel very secure about their decision, or they will needlessly feel isolated and inferior.

While our scenario does not give us the details of why Dena and Brad made the decision not to have children, we do know that it is a decision they agreed upon and we can assume, as Melody mentions, they feel secure in that choice. Shellie Arnold affirms their choice:

Important decisions, like whether or not to have children, should never be determined from past pain. In fact, it is possible that your apparent "selfishness" is really your attempt at self-preservation. Since both of you were hurt in your first marriage, deal with that issue first. You each must seek healing for your pain from God, not from each other. Then, together, you can make a decision based on God's leading and will for your home, not on what feels "safe."

Melody and Pride had postponed having children to deal with their own issues. Melody says,

For the first twelve years of our marriage, my husband and I were engrossed with completing our education and establishing our careers. We had many hurdles to cross before children could be considered. Like Dena, I brought many scars into my marriage, so I sought counseling in order to work through some of my "baggage." After really working through those issues and finally feeling ready to start a family, I found out I had fertility problems. After trying all kinds of medical intervention, we finally decided to give up. Although many people encouraged us to adopt, we felt we just were not ready. Many people looked down on us for not adopting immediately, as if our desire for a child wasn't sincere. However, we felt that we were being obedient to God's leading.

Like Melody, JoAnn and Brian feel that God has led them to the place of being a childless couple. JoAnn says,

After over seven years of infertility treatments—and failures—Brian and I also are seriously considering the *choice* of remaining childless. We believe that if it were God's will that we have children, one of the treatments would have worked. We have also concluded that if we do not have children he must have a path and purpose for our lives that could not be accomplished if we did have children. We find that prospect very exciting. We could still make the choice to defy his will and continue alternative ways to have a child and could even be successful. We believe that if we pursued that path we would not be living God's "best" life for us. Although we would not condemn anyone to face the pain of infertility, we have watched our faith grow in ways we know it would not have otherwise.

Addressing other's expectations in the decision to have children or not, Chuck says,

> All of us must strive to guide our lives with our own internal compass. It is always a mistake to live out the expectations or unfulfilled wishes of others—especially our parents. The role to produce grandchildren is perhaps the most common and powerful instance of inheriting a debt. If an individual can learn to deal with this issue successfully, all the others will be easy! To be free of the expectations of others and to live within God's will is free indeed.

While I never set out not to have children, I do believe, as do Melody and JoAnn, that remaining childless is the path God has for my life. There are many things that God has uniquely equipped me for and that I have accomplished that I could not have done if I had children. I did not have a burning desire to have children, although when I got married I assumed that I would, because that is what one did.

When Chuck and I got married we agreed to wait three years before doing anything permanent to prevent it. Three years came and we still did not feel ready to make a decision either way. We agreed to wait five years, then ten. I trust that if God wanted me to be a mother, he would have placed that desire in me so strongly that I could not ignore it. My sister, raised the same as I was, knew from childhood that she wanted to be a mom. I was a tomboy. I played with cars, not dolls. I was entrepreneurial from the time I was four years old. Today my sister has children and puppies. I have a business and cars.

In addition to my lack of maternal instincts and the true belief that I am walking the path God has set before me, I have other reasons for not pushing to have children. Many people have heard my mother's testimony and know that she lost two boys to brain damage. But few connect that story to me. Those boys were my younger brothers. Most people are unaware of the rest of our history. My grandmother, my mother's mother, lost a child in infancy. I remember talking about this with my grandmother's sister, "Aunt Jean." She was disappointed that I would choose not to have children. When I brought up the family history with her, she indignantly replied, "There was nothing the matter with Arthur."

However, seventy years ago when Arthur was born, diagnostic tests were not available as they are today. There were not always labels for diseases or illnesses. He just died. So Aunt Jean clung to the belief that there was nothing wrong with her sister's baby. We do not know. There may not have been, but there may have been some problem as well. We do know that he died in infancy.

In my generation, my sister lost a child mid-term with Down syndrome. So I have a family history of three generations of problem births. My sister has three beautiful, healthy boys. If I had felt the desire as strongly as she did to have children, I am sure that I would have—even with the history. But history confirmed my choice for me. As was stated by the wife in Jan Coleman's article, "Rarely does anyone understand."

I encourage Dena and Brad to look at their choice and why they made it. When Amanda and her husband decided not to have children, they interviewed elderly couples who didn't have children. Amanda reports,

> They are the ones who held hands and said "honey" a lot! They seemed to still be dating at seventy!

Victoria Jackson, LCSW, adds,

> It is healthier to enjoy a rich couple relationship than have children simply because it is "expected" and be resentful of the time and energy children take. Once you are a parent, you are in it for life!

Having the confidence that you have made the right choice for your life is key to dealing with the projections and expectations others put upon you. Roseanne Elling, LPC, advises,

> If the husband and the wife are both secure in the Lord about this decision, he is the foundation and peace that they can fall back on when confronted by hurtful people. Communicate the certainty of the choice to not have children with confident nonverbal cues such as looking the other person in the eye and speaking with a relaxed and confident tone of voice. Knowing you are doing God's will for your life is a huge confidence booster. People tend to accept what we say more readily if we believe it! If the husband and wife can both say "we" instead of "I" when responding, each partner will feel additional support—even in the absence of the other—and the hearer of their response will likely respect the strength of a united decision.

Kurt and Stephanie are childless by choice and are confident in their decision. Stephanie reports,

> Kurt has two daughters from his first marriage. My first marriage went bad before I really ever thought about having children. People's expectations are something

we all have to deal with. Usually the people asking the questions don't even know they are doing it. The world revolves around habits, traditions, and mindsets. If you do something out of the ordinary, you seem odd. I have learned to simply tell people the truth. If Kurt and I made a decision together for our marriage then it is our decision. Expectations do little and usually cause strife.

When a couple is confident that they've selected what's best for them—childless by choice or by acceptance—they can more easily deal with the pressures the world, the church, and the family puts on them to fit into the norm. Laura says,

> My not having children has been by choice, but it's not that way for every woman. I am satisfied with that decision, and now that I am forty-five I don't look back and regret it.

A FULL AND HAPPY LIFE

Those whose life revolves around their children look at those of us without children and know that we are missing out. Yes, we are missing out on the joys of parenting that they experience, but we can still have a full and happy life with different experiences. Jan Coleman quotes a couple, Linda and Craig, who say,

> Not everybody was meant to have children in their life. As with the whole Christian life, when you accept your situation, you can find many joys and options in it.

Having children is not what makes a marriage. In their book *Living With Infertility*, Roger and Robin Sonnenberg write,

> In words that many infertile (and childless) couples will find affirming, the late Christian counselor Walter Trobisch addressed childless marriages. Speaking to an African audience, he quoted Genesis 2:24, "Therefore, a man leaves his father and his mother and cleaves to his wife and they become one flesh." Trobisch then asked how this verse ends, and a man replied, "With a full stop," or period. Trobisch emphasized this "full stop," noting that in that key verse about marriage, a verse quoted four times in the Bible, there is not a word about children. "The effect of these words on my audience was tremendous," he recalled. "It was as if I had thrown a bomb into the church." For in the culture of those to whom he was speaking, barrenness is sufficient grounds for divorce.
>
> "Don't misunderstand me," he continued. "Children are a blessing of God." The Bible emphasizes this over and over again . . . children are a blessing to marriage, but they are an additional blessing to marriage. When God created Adam

and Eve, he blessed them and then said to them: "Be fruitful and multiply." From the Hebrew text it is clear that this commandment was an additional action to the action of blessing. Therefore, when the Bible describes the indispensable elements of marriage, it is significant that children are not expressly mentioned. Leaving, cleaving, and becoming one flesh are sufficient. Full stop. . . . The full stop means that the child does not make marriage a marriage. A childless marriage is also a marriage in the full sense of the word.[2]

Not only are couples without children in a "full marriage," as non-parent adults they can often have a positive influence on children and youth their own parents cannot have. JoAnn says,

We have found ways to connect to other children's lives that we might not have had the opportunity to do otherwise. We lavish love and gifts on our nieces and nephews and offer them one-on-one attention that they might not get at home.

Amanda found the same thing to be true in her life. She writes,

I've found that through the years I have had a profound influence on friends' children. When they wouldn't speak to their parents, they would speak to me because I was cool and not a parent. Even now, I have a sixteen-year-old girl who frequently comes over to our house, just to talk to me. Imagine, a sixteen-year-old girl wanting advice from a fifty-three-year-old woman!

Leigh and her husband related to Dena and Brad's situation. They too had faced pressure from parents and began to question their choice. In 1995 Leigh had the opportunity to go on a work camp with the teenagers from their church. She reports:

Work camp was a wonderful experience and I felt led to continue working with teenagers. Although I have to admit that it seemed a bit odd that the Lord would direct my steps to work with these young people when I had never even had a baby. I asked the Lord one day, "Why me?" His answer was that because I never wanted babies, he would give me the biggest babies of all, namely teenagers. I have worked with these young people for over five years now and taken six road trips with them, and yes, they are my babies. I love working with these kids for they give a dimension to my life that I had never known before.

She asked them why they worked together so well and was told that it was because she had never been someone's mom, just someone's kid.

They see me as a non-threatening adult—just a much older teenager. The Lord has been very gracious to my husband as well. Jim has mentored some of the young men in our church and has helped them attend the Promise Keepers meeting every year. He is respected as a spiritual leader by our young men, which I know blesses his heart as well as mine. We don't have children of our own to call us Mom and Dad, and we will never have grandchildren to call us Grandma and Grandpa, but we have spiritual children galore. We are very blessed indeed!

I feel like Leigh when she says that she has many spiritual children. Sometimes when I am asked if I have children, I say, "Yes, hundreds." I feel very maternal toward the speakers and authors I help train through the CLASSeminar. I feel like a proud mother hen each time I receive a book in the mail that has been published as a result of my involvement in the author's life. These speakers and authors are my children, even though some of them are actually older than I am and have children my age.

I remember with great fondness the influence of Aunt Jean in my life. She died at the age of ninety while I was in the midst of writing this book. I did not hesitate for a moment to drop everything and cross the country to attend her memorial service. Many of us had tears in our eyes as we shared "Aunt Jean" stories. With her as my role model, I have tried to be that kind of person for my nephews. They come and visit us for a week at a time, much as I did with Aunt Jean when I was child. Chuck and I have taken our nephews motorcycle riding, shooting, and hiking—things they do not do at home.

Chuck and I have done similar things for his nieces. His sister has been a single parent for much of her daughters' lives and their father has not been consistently involved. When Chuck's elder niece got married, she asked him to walk her down the aisle—which he was honored to do. When his younger niece was in a tough place, she came to live with us for several months. She too is now married, and some of the skills that were modeled for her in our home are now evident in hers.

Melody shares that she and her husband both remember some person in their lives who was not a parent but who had an enormous amount of influence on their lives. She says,

My husband and I feel that God has asked us to do this kind of service for kids who are already here, rather than to produce children of our own. Not everyone will understand this, and certainly not everyone is called to it. However, we feel strongly that we would not have the energy, time, or ability to do these things if we had a family of our own. Though we didn't originally think so, we are now sure that God put this path in front of us and that it is his perfect will for us. Most of the children with whom we work come from poor homes and have emotional or academic problems that severely hinder them. We don't think it is an easy task to work with them to try to help them improve—but it is a task that brings us great joy!

Chuck reminds Dena and Brad, and all childless couples, that there are so many children and teens in need of adults who are willing to make an investment in them. Many technically "childless" teachers, counselors, social workers, youth ministers, and extended family members are making a greater contribution to the next generation than some parents. It is not the genetic material contributed that counts, it's the sum contribution to the welfare and Christian upbringing of the children that matters.

Perhaps you can benefit from the advice for Dena and Brad; search your heart before God and ask him what his path is for your life. As you can tell from the sampling of stories shared here, it may be his plan that you not have children. But don't hold back on the extravagant love he has placed within you. Great joy is out there for you. The maternal instinct doesn't stop at your own doorstep.

Interaction

1. Write out a list of expectations others have of you, including who expressed (or implied) them.

2. Evaluate each expectation and who it came from for validity. Challenge each expectation, asking yourself, "Does this person have a right to set expectations for my life?" "Am I honoring this person's expectations out of my desires or out of guilt?"

3. Write out your expectations of each other as husband and wife. As a couple, these expectations are to be taken very seriously. Discuss them as a couple to be sure individual assumptions are accurate.

4. Write out your expectations of yourself. Each one has to be tested for validity to determine that it is truly your own rather than an expectation someone else has for you.

5. Write out your heart's desire and any call(s) felt—God's expectations for your life. Read *You've Got What It Takes* for additional guidance on God's will for your life.

6. Fill in the blank: "My life is missing _____." Make plans to meet that missing need.

7. Review what God has called you to do and your expectations of each other. These are to be your priority. Everyone else's expectations (if valid) are secondary.

Chapter SEVENTEEN

The Fire's Gone Out

Personality Differences, Physical Relationship

The Issue

*T*odd is a Peaceful Phlegmatic and a schoolteacher. Erica is a Powerful Choleric, although most of her life she has functioned in her role as a Perfect Melancholy, her secondary personality. Todd and Erica were high school sweethearts in their small town. They came from traditional homes, married young, and reproduced their parents' marriages. Todd settled into being the breadwinner, while Erica managed the home. Erica became pregnant with their first child on their honeymoon. Two more children quickly followed. Erica was a good mother and used her natural abilities to manage the family in an enviable manner.

When the youngest reached high school, Erica found she had time on her hands for the first time since her own childhood. She began taking classes in real estate, and within two years she had become the top producer in her area.

As she competed in the business world, she adopted the characteristics of other professionals. She developed her Powerful Choleric Personality and took on the fast-talking, multitasking, cell-phone-packing style so dominant in our culture. The money rolled in.

Meanwhile Todd labored away in the public schools, unappreciated and underpaid. In comparison, his modest salary seemed inferior to Erica's commissioned sales income.

In social settings Todd went from respected educator and leader of a beautiful family to "Aren't you the husband of Erica, the million-dollar producer?" Todd felt he had lost his role as provider and leader of the family.

All of this took a toll on the couple's sex life. Erica confided in her best friend, saying, "Todd hasn't touched me in months." Todd found the "new Erica" threatening and unattractive. As he withdrew and sulked, Erica found him increasingly unappealing.

There are confident men at Erica's office, and there are pretty young teachers at Todd's school. A potential crisis!

Insights

Todd and Erica are at the place where many couples who have had a stable marriage for years find their relationship struggling. Kris commented,

> This is such a typical twist in a marriage. Pete and I are going through a somewhat similar situation. Although I haven't yet finished my education for a new role in life, I see Pete winding down after a successful career and looking for home time—which is all I ever had!

Chuck frequently saw this dynamic while working with military couples after retirement. For twenty years the wife supported the career of the husband, moving every two or three years. After retirement the wife says, "Now it's my turn." But it is hard for the "old soldier" to change.

We often see a marriage that has appeared to be good and solid for fifteen to twenty-five years suddenly crumble when the family roles shift. People look on from the outside and wonder what happened. In reality, rather than living the happy marriage everyone thought they had, they simply had developed a lifestyle in which they had grown comfortable. Todd and Erica's relationship had the predictability of Ozzie and Harriet. They had developed an equilibrium that gave them a sense of stability and balance.

As a Peaceful Phlegmatic, we can assume that Todd was comfortable with the routine his homelife had taken on. However, as a Powerful Choleric with some Perfect Melancholy, Erica was ready for a change. She was ready to spread her wings and develop her gifts outside of her role as a wife and mother. Anytime a relationship undergoes such a major shift in the equilibrium as Todd and Erica's did, there are bound to be problems that arise during the adjustment period. Georgia Shaffer, Pennsylvania-licensed psychologist, says,

> Major changes, as Erica and Todd experienced, can upset the status quo of any marriage. They need time to let go of what was, time to readjust, and time to begin anew.

While there are many aspects of the relationship that could be discussed, several are well covered in other chapters. If this scenario relates to your situation, please be sure to read the following chapters, as much of their content will also apply: "Bet the Farm" (3), "Orchestrate Finances" (7), and "Lack of Time Together" (2). These chapters address issues such as finding one's self-worth in God rather than employment, combining incomes, and creating quality time together. The two issues that are applicable to Todd and Erica that we will cover here are their Personality differences and their physical relationship.

PERSONALITY DIFFERENCES

Because Erica made the changes, she is the one whose actions knocked the equilibrium out of balance in the marriage. She will have to put in the most effort to help establish a new center. In response to this situation, Roseanne Elling, LPC, says,

> This marriage needs some reprioritizing, especially on the part of Erica. She may have to choose her marriage ("us") over her career ("me") at times.

Some casual onlookers might say that Erica needs to scale back her job and spend more time being "Mom." After all, life seemed good for the marriage then. Some may even go so far as to say that Erica is wrong to be working outside the home at all. On the other side, the more feminist view would declare that Erica should have spread her wings a long time ago, and after so many years of caring for her children she deserves "her turn." As is usually the case with extreme viewpoints, somewhere in the middle is probably more appropriate. Neither extreme will save the marriage; either will leave one party—Erica or Todd—unhappy with the relationship. This is where the love extravagantly principle comes into play: not doing what seems "fair" but what is right for the health of the marriage.

We know that Erica is a Powerful Choleric, though these traits took a backseat during her prime mothering years. As such, we assume that her need for leadership, control, and recognition have been boiling below the surface, waiting to get out for many years. Consequently telling her to quit her job and go back to being a full-time mom would only solve the problem on the outside, leaving Erica champing at the bit.

A friend of mine found herself in a similar situation. Her two children were grown and out of the house. She began a new career that utilized her natural skills and personality. Her daughter was of a very conservative mindset and had a traditional marriage. While my friend and her husband had no trouble with her new work, her daughter did! My friend asked her daughter what she was supposed to do with her time now that she wasn't raising children. The daughter thought she should "serve in a soup kitchen" or something similar—a worthwhile pursuit if her mother's gifts had been in that area.

For Erica, real estate is a good option, as it allows flexibility to be available when her youngest son needs her. The issue comes for Erica in meeting her needs without ignoring her husband's.

If Erica were to come to her for counsel, Ruth Kopp, M.D., says,

> First I would ask Erica what she wants. Does she want to be right, to be vindicated, to have me agree that she is entitled to her career success? Or does she want her marriage revitalized and a right relationship with her husband? If she wants to be "right," there is no real hope for the marriage.

Georgia Shaffer comments along the same theme:

> It sounds like each has been hurt. Unless some important changes are made and forgiveness is practiced, they may find themselves drifting further apart.

While the scenario doesn't state a Christian commitment, we can assume that both Todd and Erica are Christians. As such, they know that divorce is never God's perfect plan, and they desire to make their marriage work. Both will need to make some changes, both will need to be willing to love extravagantly—not to get, but to give.

Before Todd and Erica can look at the presenting problem: "He hasn't touched me in months," they need to address their relationship. Shellie Arnold has a lay ministry promoting intimacy in couples. She states,

> Intimacy is what happens when our hearts, emotions, minds, and spirits are functioning properly, with or without sex. Todd and Erica's sex life is suffering because their intimate life is suffering.

To begin to build up their relationship, each needs to gain an understanding of their Personalities and the emotional needs that accompany the way God created them. Victoria Jackson, LCSW, recommends:

> [Erica and Todd], you need to consider studying the Personality styles each of you are and note how you have changed since the beginning of your marriage. Celebrate the differences. View it as an exciting aspect of your relationship.

For strong women who are married to men who have quieter Personalities, the contrast seems exaggerated as society, especially the church, expects the man to be the leader and the woman the follower. When this is not the way we are wired, as in the case of Erica and Todd, we women need to put forth the extra effort to understand and lift up our husband.

Ruth Kopp, who faces a similar Personality combination in her marriage, says,

The Powerful Choleric will usually be the one to take the initiative in learning to "speak Peaceful Phlegmatic" and will need to be willing to initiate change and make the majority of changes.

Diane agrees with Dr. Kopp:

As someone who is in the "reverse" role in later married life, I can relate to the upset in balance. I believe it's incumbent on the wife to try to ensure that her husband is feeling needed and wanted by her. Oftentimes we appear so self-sufficient that our husbands think they don't have anything to give us anymore and that they are not our number-one priority (and often, they're not). Peaceful Phlegmatics don't realize that as they withdraw they become more annoying to the Powerful Choleric and less attractive, perpetuating a downward cycle. My experience is that the wife must go out of her way to assure her husband that she still values him.

Being willing to take this first step is where the love extravagantly concept becomes important.

Chuck and I have a similar personality combination in that I am more the up-front person, more the leader. He is content in the background and shuns the spotlight. I long for social activity and a large network of friends. He is happy with one or two friendships that have developed over decades. Like Erica, I am in the business world. Chuck and Todd are not. Chuck as a therapist and Todd as a teacher, function in the world of the arts and sciences. I have had to learn to adjust to his needs. I used to come home in what Chuck called "boss mode"—with my Powerful Choleric traits dominant. He often had to remind me that he was not one of my employees. This side of me highlighted my less attractive traits that were particularly unattractive to Chuck.

Because I love Chuck and want to make our marriage work, and because I understand our personality differences, I have been able to modify my behavior—especially when I am with him.

Georgia Shaffer cautions Erica,

Although your success is a boost for your ego, you need to be careful not to ride the waves of success at the expense of your husband's self-esteem.

I have made a conscious decision to love Chuck extravagantly, to make changes in my approach that boost Chuck and his self-esteem.

When Nance married my Uncle Ron, she was already known and successful as a real estate agent. However, he was a popular radio personality, used to acclaim. I remember her saying that when she is with him, she views her job as carrying the spotlight and shining it on him. It takes a secure woman to be willing to set aside her success and/or fame to shine the spotlight on her husband, but this is what I try to do and it is exactly what Erica needs to do. Melanie Wilson, Ph.D., agrees:

> Erica and Todd need to praise one another in front of friends and family as well.

So first I'd encourage Erica to understand Todd's Peaceful Phlegmatic Personality. He thrives on stability and does not like change. One of the deep-seated emotional needs of the Peaceful Phlegmatic is respect and a feeling of self worth. In the years prior to this crisis, Todd had a stable life. He has lived in the same town. He has lived with the same woman. He has had the same job. He probably expected to come home and find dinner ready, which we can assume happened. He also had respect and a feeling of self worth. He was the breadwinner. His higher education and position as a "respected educator" fed his needs. Now he feels trivialized.

On the other hand, Erica's Powerful Choleric Personality thrives on change and excitement. She loves a flurry of activity and is a natural leader. Two of her inborn emotional needs are for achievement and appreciation for all she does. Once her children grew beyond their intense daily need for her time and attention, she sought new avenues for achievement. Her success in real estate is giving her that achievement and the rewards fill her need for appreciation.

As she understands Todd's Personality, Erica can love him extravagantly by making adjustments to minimize the upheaval and change her career has brought into his life. She can draw upon her Perfect Melancholy strengths when she is with him, tone down her voice, and maintain the order at home to which he is accustomed. Roseanne Elling tells of some friends of hers who are in a similar situation, but have learned what the other needs:

> The Powerful Choleric wife pays attention to some little things, such as how her Peaceful Phlegmatic husband likes the towels in the bathroom folded. She takes time to do the things she knows are important to him. Although she is busy and is a top producer in her field, her attention to the his desires makes him feel that he is important to her.

Both in private and in public, Erica needs to shine the spotlight on Todd. This is apt to take some real effort on her part, but if her true desire is to love Todd with extravagance, through the power of the Holy Spirit, she can do it. The difficulty is that as a Powerful Choleric, Erica respects strength. After being out in the business community with high-visibility men whose activities command respect, Todd looks dull and boring—not strong. Melanie Wilson suggests that if Todd were to share with Erica how he feels about making a difference in the lives of his students, despite his low salary, Erica may view him in a new perspective. Erica needs to be able to feel proud of Todd and the work he does, his achievements and accomplishments.

In making the attitude adjustment to feel proud of her husband, Ruth Kopp says,

> I am more Powerful Choleric than my husband in regard to work and business. His Perfect Melancholy tendencies slow me down and I can choose to be impatient with them and brush them aside (and end up being sorry!) or I can see that God has put him in my life precisely to slow me down and make me think! When I remember to check with him before making business decisions, I make better decisions, and we are a team.

Reflecting on her friends' situation, Roseanne Elling says,

> She is very proud of what he does and talks about it, much more than she talks about her own work in social situations. I believe she is comfortable with herself and gets enough acclaim for her success at work, so she doesn't feel like she's competing when she's at home or out socially. Her admiration of her Peaceful Phlegmatic husband's character and his personal job success, although it is very different from hers, is obvious to all who are around them. He feels respected by her.

Eva Marie has found this technique to be effective in her marriage. She reports,

> I so identify with this couple. For years I have run my household, complete with children and pets, as a Perfect Melancholy. Everything was in order! Everything had an order. My husband, a Peaceful Phlegmatic, was and is happy doing his job, coming home, and being a husband and father. Now that the kids are grown and gone, he is excited about spending the rest of our lives in quiet solitude.
>
> Now that we are at that "empty nest" crossroads, the opportunity for me to see my lifelong dream of being a published author has finally come to pass. Mr. Peaceful Phlegmatic couldn't be happier for me . . . and, as long as he doesn't have to attend too many public functions, he is just fine. But now my Powerful

Choleric side is *really* surfacing, and we are having the difficulties of his wanting a quiet life and my wanting a driven one.

Working through this has been a true test of faith! The most important thing for me has been to recognize his need for *my time* . . . away from the computer, the phones, the paperwork, etc. Every day I should have time set aside just for him and no one else.

While Erica may need to be the one to take the first step, both will need to make some adjustments to save their marriage. Georgia Shaffer advises,

Erica and Todd need to be cautious and affirm each other rather than look for affirmation in the people at work. It is so easy to be pulled in by the encouragement and compliments of those who don't have to live with us week in and week out. Many people don't plan to have affairs, but before they know it they are emotionally swept away by the steady dose of attention and compliments.

In understanding that as a Powerful Choleric Erica needs appreciation for all she does, Todd can make new efforts to appreciate and admire her skills and abilities—this is where love extravagantly will come into play for him. Andrea Golzmane, MA, LMFT, says,

We all resist change, especially when the relationship itself changes so much as functions change. The sign of a healthy marriage is the willingness for people to be flexible and to "step out of the box" and create something new in the relationship.

Marj is an attorney with a background in real estate. She is a Powerful Choleric married to a Peaceful Phlegmatic. From her experience, Marj suggests the following:

Erica deserves to spread her wings and fly, especially after years of tending children and home, but she cannot do so at the expense of her marriage. She needs to watch carefully the time she gives her husband, and make sure that he gets a fair dose of quality time.

Todd needs to be supportive of his wife. She gave up "flying" for years to tend to the family and home. He needs to get involved with her job. He will find that there is a lot to do, and that his help will be greatly appreciated by his wife. They will then be more of a team, and can enjoy together the fruits of their labor. When introduced as "Erica's husband," Erica can say proudly that without Todd she could not have done it (rather than that her success came in spite of him).

His help could include going with her to open houses. During times when no one is there, they can be together. When many people are there, he can be of assistance answering questions, being friendly, etc.

Ruth Kopp encourages Erica to involve Todd in her business. She says,

If Erica wants Todd's input in her life and business, she will have to plan ahead and think before she asks for it, otherwise she'll overwhelm him and discourage him. The key here is to be aware of the fact that Todd's input is helpful and valuable, and that it is definitely worth making the personal changes that give her access to his thinking, support, and advice.

As Erica and Todd begin to understand each other's Personality and make adjustments in their relationship accordingly, they will begin to find each other more appealing. In reviewing the situation, Andrea Golzmane says,

They have grown apart in that Todd feels set aside as the head of the house and Erica feels unwanted as a female.

Before addressing the issues of sex, Roseanne Elling reminds them that they are a team: "It's very difficult to feel romantic when you're competing." Stephanie agrees,

If they can work on what they are doing as a team, the sex problems and temptations may not be a factor at all.

PHYSICAL RELATIONSHIP

Erica has complained that Todd has not "touched her in months." As we have seen, their relationship needs work before they even look at the sexual issues. Once they learn to meet each other's differing emotional needs, the sex issues may take care of themselves. As they rediscover each other and make an effort to enjoy one another again, they are creating an environment of affection. In his book *His Needs, Her Needs,* Willard Harley states, "Affection is the environment of the marriage and sex is the special event."[1] Everything we have discussed up to this point is about creating that environment. Now to the special event.

Here both spouses can do things spiritually, physically, and emotionally to set the stage for intimacy, but again, the wife can lead in this area. Diane addressed this beautifully:

Our husbands also need to know that we desire them. We can purpose in our hearts to create romantic interludes with our husbands. Be playful, soft, vulnerable. Bottom line—the relationship between husband and wife is ultimately far more valuable than a successful career. If we take as much time to cultivate this mentality with our husbands as we do in being successful, we can experience the greatest success in both arenas!

I love her idea of using our success mindset to be successful in this aspect of our lives as well. We Powerful Choleric women love a good challenge. Making sex a special event after a damaged relationship will be a challenge, but one that can be conquered. It will be worth the effort!

The place for Erica to start is with prayer. She needs to pray for an attitude adjustment so that she will be willing to take the physical and emotional steps to improve their sex life. In responding to Erica's situation, Suzy offered the following:

Whenever I have found my husband "unappealing," I have done two things. First, I pray about my sex life. I know this sounds simple, but many times we do not ask God for help. I started praying about my sexual experience when my husband went through a depression many years ago, and he didn't seem to be the man I married. Whew! If God doesn't honor our prayers! He created sex and knows how to make it what it was intended to be! The next thing I did was try to recreate the things that sexually attracted me in the first place to my husband. We love to work out together, so we found time to play together by swimming, running, and playing tennis. After that, I saw him in a whole different light.

Shellie Arnold advises further:

In the Garden of Eden, before sin entered the world and Adam and Eve's marriage, Scripture tells us, "And the man and his wife were both naked and were not embarrassed or ashamed in each other's presence" (Genesis 2:25 AMP). Todd and Erica will have to work to strip the stress and persona of the day away and get reconnected physically. They should hold each other naked in bed and pray, "Father, help this be a fun, healing, and fulfilling time for both of us. Re-bless our union." Then with their hearts placed in God's hands, they should let their hands roam and their hormones rage to love and rediscover each other. God loves to help lovemaking become more fruitful and enjoyable for his children. After all, it was his idea and his plan in the first place.

Prayer is the best place to start. In her book *The Power of a Praying Wife*, Stormie Omartian suggests the following prayer:

Lord, bless my husband's sexuality and make it an area of great fulfillment for him. Restore what needs to be restored, balance what needs to be balanced. Protect us from apathy, disappointment, criticism, busyness, unforgiveness, deadness, or disinterest. I pray that we make time for one another, communicate our true feelings openly, and remain sensitive to each other's needs.[2]

One thing that may be helpful for Erica to realize is that at this phase of life sex is probably not going to be what it was on the honeymoon. After reading of Erica and Todd's situation, Mallory wrote,

> Sex, now let me think . . . what was that like? A few years ago I went to my dentist—a 100 percent Popular Sanguine woman. While waiting I skimmed *Parade Magazine* and read its decade report on the sex profile of Americans. When my dentist's hand was out of my mouth, I shared what I had read with her. It said the middle-aged group had sex seven times a month—we both died laughing . . . wondering who did it that many times when we were all working and exhausted and couldn't care less? Somehow the pace of living has us fall into bed together, hug, snuggle, and fall asleep. . . . However, I can honestly say that our relationship is much better when we *do* have sex! It really does bring a sense of intimacy like nothing else does.

Like Erica and Todd, Cassie's marriage is in a role reversal stage as well. She reports,

> Lovemaking is less frequent, but definitely more tender. When we do make love, it generally starts out slower and builds. In this period of life, I have found that the danger for older couples, even with intimate conversation and sharing, can be feeling more like brothers and sisters than lovers. This is another reason to continue to seek a healthy and satisfying relationship.

Yes, sex does change in different phases of a couple's life, but it can be fanned into flame again. There are many nights when falling into bed together, hugging, snuggling, and falling asleep is the best Chuck and I can do. Yet when we are on vacation, the statistics are totally different. During a week in St. Thomas we walked hand in hand on the beach. We went snorkeling. We had fun dinners together. We sat on the balcony of our room and watched the sunset. Without the stresses and cares of daily life, that honeymoon quality was rediscovered. We have found similar results at a nearby bed and breakfast and at a friend's borrowed mountain cabin.

When Chuck works with couples, he coaches them to begin looking at long- and short-term priorities. When asked, most of us would order our priorities: God, spouse, children, and so on. Yet on a day-to-day basis our lives are filled with short-term trivia. If the gas gauge on the car says empty, we put gas in the car now or it will grind to a stop. Often we go days, weeks, or even years without putting any gas into the marriage. Because the intimate relationship can wait, it never comes up as a priority unless we truly make it one.

Addressing the importance of making the sexual relationship a priority, Stormie Omartian writes,

> After twenty years of praying with women about their failing, struggling, unful-filling, or dead marriages, I've observed that frequently the sexual relationship is a low priority. It isn't that the wife cares nothing about that part of her life. It's that there are so many other things screaming for her attention, such as raising children, work, finances, managing a home, emotional stress, exhaustion, sickness, and marital strife. In the wife's juggling of priorities, sex can end up at the bottom of her list. Some women allow week after week, month after month, six months a year to go by without having sexual relations with their husbands for one reason or another. When disaster hits, they are surprised.[3]

Erica and Todd need to take some time away to have fun and focus on each other. Evelyn Davison is known as the "Christian Dr. Ruth" in Austin, Texas, where her daily radio program "LoveTalk" airs. She advises Todd and Erica:

> When the passion flickers low, take a day or weekend off to spend time together without phones or beepers. Do something that was fun when you first got mar-ried. Forget the kids at school and the clients at the office. After the physical fun activity (not sexual), separate for at least an hour and write out a "things I have always loved about you" list. Then meet again somewhere with an atmosphere conducive to conversation like a coffee house or a bluff overlooking the city and take turns sharing the list of "I love yous." This can help move you to compassion for the needs of each other. The surprise comes when the passion returns. It may not be as hot as it was on the honeymoon sexual encounter, but it should be lively!

If finances or responsibilities dictate that a week in the Caribbean is not feasible, look for other options. Perhaps friends have a cabin in the mountains that can provide the same type of getaway—away from the cares of the world and into the world of each other. Erica and Todd may need to start with more than a day—a full weekend—together or, better yet, a week. Victoria Jackson suggests,

> Erica can make suggestions that they take a weekend away to reconnect. She can express a need to be with him—husbands like to feel desired too!

After an extended period of time away from the dailyness of life to reconnect—emotionally, physically, and spiritually—Todd and Erica will need to make
specific plans to keep the flame fanned once they are back into their routine at
home. Talking about her own marriage, Jane says,

> While I am not rich, famous, or powerful, I do make more money than my
> husband and probably have more social contacts. My advice to Todd and Erica is
> to designate a weekly date night where they can cast aside their cares and truly
> focus on each other.

Creative time together is discussed more completely in chapter 2, "Lack of Time
Together."

Whether or not they are on a "date," Chuck encourages Erica to leave the
office persona at the office. When she comes home, she needs to make a conscious
effort to switch into her role of wife and mother. This may involve turning off the
cell phone, taking off the "gold jacket," and mentally slowing down. Something as
simple as a change of clothing can impact a mental shift.

From her work as a lay minister with couples, Stephanie Janke asks,

> What about a different hat? During our small group study we made crowns to
> wear. The men's said *Honor and Respect* across the front, while the women's said
> *Love and Cherish*. We found that during difficult times, putting on the crowns not
> only reminded us of the importance of our roles as husband and wife, but also
> added a little fun to lighten up any tension that was building.

While clothing can be important, the rest of our surroundings can be as well.
Chuck's undergraduate degree is in motion picture production. From this background he suggests that Todd and Erica "dress the set," meaning to make their
bedroom a place conducive to making love. When couples come to Chuck with
sexual problems in their marriage, he has learned to ask, "Do you have an ironing
board and a basket of laundry in the bedroom?" More often than not, the answer
is yes. There may be a computer on a desk next to the bed or other paraphernalia
that has nothing to do with what goes on in a bedroom. While household space
may cause limitations for some couples, as much as possible prepare the bedroom
for a romantic interlude.

I remember hearing my mother speak on the topic of marriage when I was a
teenager. She asked the women in her audience, "If your husband was going to
have an affair today, while you are here at this conference, would he do it in your
bedroom in the condition you left it this morning?" An audible gasp was heard
throughout the crowd, as most had left an unmade bed, baskets of laundry, an

ironing board, and more, cluttering the bedroom. The point, of course, was not to prepare the bedroom for your husband to have an affair with another woman, but to keep it in a condition where he will want to have one with you!

Erica should pray a prayer like the one found in Stormie Omartian's book *The Power of a Praying Wife*:

> Help me to create a peaceful, restful, safe place for him to come home to. Teach me to take care of myself and stay attractive to him. Grow me into a creative and confident woman who is rich in mind, soul and spirit. Make me the kind of woman he can be proud to say is his wife.[4]

As Erica takes steps to invite Todd to make love, he too needs to make Erica feel needed and feminine. Chuck suggests that Todd purchase feminine lingerie and perfume for her. Sweep her off her feet!

As Erica and Todd love each other with extravagance, setting aside what is fair and doing what is right for their marriage, they will find that the fire has not gone completely out. There are embers that can be stirred and brought back to life. Roseanne Elling says,

> Couples mistakenly believe that the fire of the honeymoon continues to roar on its own. The truth is that it burns inconsistently, sometimes flaring up, sometimes burning steadily, and sometimes waning into mere embers. It's up to both partners to keep the fire burning, and it takes effort!

The Interaction

1. Both husband and wife need to alternate days as the initiator of intimacy. Relationships tend to fall into a pursuer/distancer dynamic. The longer each member of the couple remains in the same role, the further the couple tends to grow apart. By reversing roles frequently, the couple grows together. The husband might take odd days, the wife taking the even. Being the pursuer means initiating intimacy with touch, kisses, hugs, saying, "I love you," etc.

2. The husband is to buy, gift wrap, and present intimate attire that is sexy, yet tasteful. He should rehearse the compliments he will offer his wife when she is wearing his selection that will make her know he finds her attractive—and deliver them when they are together. "Not bad" and "Okay" are not acceptable praise.

3. The wife will take responsibility to "dress the set" (bedroom). She will plan an evening of intimacy. Her actions might include personal pampering, new sheets, candles, a bubbly beverage, wearing the new intimate apparel, music, meeting her husband at the door, etc.

4. After a successful evening at home, the husband is to plan and execute an intimate surprise overnight getaway. He should pack for both (perhaps involving the assistance of her closest friend to ensure he remembers everything important to her) and arrange for childcare if needed.

5. Both partners need to develop a "language of intimacy" that will allow them to address sexual needs and desires comfortably. This builds on the basic skills outlined in the communication exercise found in appendix D. However, while the exercise focuses on communicating emotional needs, the "language of intimacy" is directed more toward physical needs. To initiate the use of the "language of inti-macy" and become more comfortable talking about physical needs and desires, the couple may start with a back rub that over a period of time evolves into a full body massage, including intimate areas, alternating spouses as the recipient.

From the Head to the Heart

Willingness to Change

As you continue to use this book, I trust that you are encouraged to know that you are not alone. Many couples face circumstances similar to the ones you are going through. It is my desire that reading about others who have gone through difficulties, and lived through them, will offer you hope. Those who contributed their personal stories were eager to help someone else traveling down the same road. While your situation may look like you are in a dark tunnel, those who have been there before are reaching back, giving you their hand to guide you to the light on the other side.

Reading a book like this can make you aware that there is an issue in your marriage and that it has a solution. Reading a book can give you hope. But to apply what you learn, to see a difference in your situation, takes more than hope. It takes a desire and willingness to change.

Love Extravagantly is full of plans and projects. You can read them. You can close the book and put it on a shelf. While I appreciate your buying the book, and I am grateful that you read it, I wrote it to help you. I assume that you bought this book because you have a need. Perhaps you heard me speak and liked my direct, practical approach. You went to the book table at that event and saw this book.

The title and cover design made you pick it up. You read the back cover copy and decided it was something you needed.

Reading the previous pages, you may have seen symptoms similar to ones reflected in your marriage. Like the marriages described here, you too have a modern marriage. You too have some complications from which you'd like relief. Reading the scenarios and insights may have brought up issues that you had not yet thought about. But what is important is what you do from here. It is all about change.

This is the main reason people buy self-help or personal-growth books. This is the reason people seek counseling. They desire relief from their symptoms or from the consequences of their actions. With the plethora of therapists and types of counseling available and the proliferation of self-help books and tapes out there, no one should have any problems at all. Yet problems are clearly prevalent. After being involved in marriage accountability groups for the past four years, Kurt and Stephanie Janke have found that even the best marriages have problems. "Maybe they aren't giants, but they are little quills that prick us now and then and make us realize things could be different."

The Theory of Change

People read books and close the cover. They may even mean to apply the ideas that sparked their interest. A change may occur for a few weeks and then most people slip back into their previous patterns.

People go for counseling. They affirm the adjustments. In front of the counselor they agree to the approach. They walk out the door and go right back to their old ways.

Does this make self-help books wrong? Does this mean that counseling is ineffective? No. But it does mean that for you to see real changes in your marriage relationship, for you to make the reading of this book more than a simple exercise, it must go from your head to your heart. You must have a real desire for a changed heart.

We see the same thing happening in the church. Last week Franklin Graham preached a powerful and compelling sermon in our service. While our pastor does an altar call almost every week, the response to Franklin was much greater. Evangelism is his gift. But what will happen to those people who went forward in response to Franklin's message? They may have responded out of a fear of consequences. Many people come forward, but few see a true reordering of their life.

The "Sunday Christians" come to church each week. They bring their Bibles, sing the songs, and underline passages. They know enough Scripture to be convicted, but not enough to be transformed. They know they should change and that church attendance is a good thing. Yet Sunday Christians revert back to their old ways as soon as the pressure is off because the change is only on the surface, only in their head. Family Systems Theory calls this first-order change, done for appearances or symptom relief. Does this make church a bad thing? Does this mean that Christianity is ineffective? No. But it does mean that the truly changed life takes more than church attendance. Those who have made a real commitment to their Christian walk have been reborn in the Spirit. They change not out of fear of the consequences of their actions but out of a desire for a changed heart.

The same process is evident in physical fitness. We know we should get into better shape, so we buy equipment or join a fitness club. Club memberships take a big jump at the first of the year, because that is when people make a commitment to get into shape. Trying to find space on a Stairmaster in January is difficult. Come March, there is plenty of opportunity. Friends in the business tell me that health clubs count on people buying a membership and then only using it sporadically at best. Garage sales are weighted with rowing machines, tummy toners, treadmills, and other equipment bought with the best of intentions. But after years of dusting it or hanging laundry on it, someone gives up and decides to sell the reminder of the failure. Does this mean that getting into shape is a bad idea? Should we all just accept our out-of-shape condition? No.

Creating a Change in Your Life

Whether talking about our health, our faith, or our marriage, instituting change is hard work. We need to go beyond the head, beyond first-order change—not seeking change merely for symptom relief, but from a desire born of a changed heart. Hard work can bring about second-order change and the reordering of a person's life.

To bring about this level of change usually requires constant reimmersion. Going to the health club once will not change your physique. Even sporadic visits will produce no visible effects. However, a regular routine—reordering your life— is effective. Going to church on Christmas and Easter does not create a new person. Even weekly Sunday attendance is no guarantee. However, a real relationship with God that happens day in and day out does bring about change on the heart level resulting in a reordered life. Similarly, reading a book will not give you an improved marriage.

Because this deeper level of change requires a reordering of your life, each of the chapters has been presented in a clear problem/solution format. We desire—

and know it is possible from those who read the manuscript in its developmental stages—that as you read the scenarios and consider your own situation, you project your own marriage into the setting. Then as you read over the suggested solutions, the Interactions, you will see how to apply these answers to your own situation.

Chuck strongly suggests that you reread the applicable chapters with your spouse. If your particular issue is different from any presented, use a chapter as a model to formulate your own chapter. Together write out what a therapist like Chuck would call a problem statement. This is a judgment-free description of the issue that reflects the perspectives of both parties. The problem statement does not place blame on either party and describes the situation as an unbiased observer would see it—objective and free of criticism. This model helps you view the issue from a solution-focused perspective, moving you from blame to solution. Chances are it will reflect the scenarios addressed in *Love Extravagantly*, but as every marriage is unique, your problem statement will be different from another couple's with a similar situation.

Next, write out what the issue will look like when it gets better. We call this a "compass statement" as it guides you to the end point. For example, using a few of the scenarios from the previous pages, a problem statement might be "Louise resents their money going to the ex-spouse" or "The marriage lacks connectedness, instead it feels more like a business." After discussion, the description of what it will look like when the problem is better, the compass statement, might be "The ex-wife is no longer a divisive issue; the issue changes to a challenge they face together." Or "We will know the marriage is better when the 'two are one flesh' concept is in evidence: both parties agree that the value of the marital bond exceeds the value of material assets."

Once you have developed your problem statement and your compass statement, a good counselor or other wise advisor can help you brainstorm different hypotheses on why the issue exists. This hypothesis would point toward how to tackle the issue. Using the same scenario, the hypothesis might be "Out of guilt and a desire to pacify his ex-wife, Darren agreed to a divorce settlement without the benefit of legal counsel. In order to avoid conflict or guilt, Darren continues to write 'one more check' each month. The long-term consequence of this financial drain is a building resentment in Louise." Or "Less than full commitment to the marriage and the blending of two independent or conflicting money management systems are discouraging interconnectedness in the marital relationship."

Once you have created the problem statement, the compass statement, and the hypothesis or hypotheses that will help clarify the situation, then select a solution, or "insights" for action, that tests—confirming or disproving—the validity of the hypothesis. Often developing a solution brings about change with movement toward the compass statement. In other cases, different solutions to the problem must be thought out, tried, and evaluated. If you are trying to develop these statements on your own, be sure to seek the wise counsel of friends, family, or others who know you—such as your pastor.

Throughout the pages of *Love Extravagantly*, we have presented various possible solutions for a variety of situations. Bringing together a team of experts to review each scenario, we have brainstormed and developed several premises throughout each chapter—called "Insights." As the two of you review the appropriate scenarios and relate them to your own life, select the solution that most closely reflects your needs and will bring about the desired change. Review this process, reimmersing yourself in it frequently to see how you are progressing. Change can be measured by how far you have moved toward the compass statement, your definition of "better."

Because reordering your life, bringing about second-order change, does take work—like getting in better physical health or developing a stronger spiritual life—there are exercises called "Interaction" at the end of each chapter. These activities will help keep you focused on your process of change. Do not skip over them if you hope to see a true change of heart. Go back and, using a journal or blank paper, work through the exercises. Write your own interaction; be creative!

Being willing to make these deeper changes is what the principle of *Love Extravagantly* is all about. You change your heart attitude from getting to giving:

> Observe how Christ loved us. His love is not cautious but extravagant. He didn't love in order to get something from us but to give everything of himself to us. Love like that. (Ephesians 5:1–2 THE MESSAGE)

In her book *Having a Mary Heart in a Martha World*, Joanna Weaver speaks of extravagant love. She writes,

> That's extravagant love. The kind of love that disregards everything else so it can focus on one thing alone: the object of that love. The kind of love that sacrifices everything, only wishing it had more to give. Nothing is too precious. Nothing is too exorbitant. The heart demands that we give—and give all.[1]

Some people will be strong enough and disciplined enough to make this heart-level change on their own, just like the few regulars who show up at the gym, do their routine, and see results. But most will need some form of assistance and accountability. A book like *Love Extravagantly* may be all the assistance some people need. In their quest for improved health, some have a strong enough desire for change that they only need one visit with the trainer to show them what to do. From there they carry on. Others will need good nourishment to aid their progress, and still others will need regular visits with a trainer or coach to help them stay on track. I liken this process to the health club environment because it is easy to see the different levels of progress and help. If a person truly desires to make changes in their physical well-being, they need more than lifting weights, more than working out. They need good nourishment.

For those with the goal of improved marital health, this book is like your initial visit with your personal trainer, giving you hope and getting you on the right track. The good nourishment is the power of the Holy Spirit and the Word of God. Human nature blinds us to our own issues. We can read about them, see steps that would be helpful, but skip right over them, choosing to believe that they do not apply to us. We do this with Scripture. We can read passages many times without their having an impact our lives. But through the power of the Holy Spirit, we may read the verse and see it appear in a whole new light. It seems to jump off the page and hit us in the face. This is what happened for me when I read through Ephesians and came to "love extravagantly." Romans 8:5 affirms this:

> For those who live according to the flesh have their outlook shaped by the things of the flesh, but those who live according to the Spirit have their outlook shaped by the things of the Spirit (NET).

Before you and your spouse go through *Love Extravagantly* again, and read the scenarios that are applicable to you, be prayerful together. Ask God to help you remove any denial that may be present in your part of the issue. Ask him to cause the situations that apply to you to "hit you in the face." John 14:26 promises us that he can do this for us. "The Holy Spirit, whom the Father will send in My name, He will teach you all things, and bring to your remembrance all things . . ." (NKJV). Oswald Chambers describes it this way,

> We think we understand another person's struggle until God reveals the same shortcomings in our lives. There are vast areas of stubbornness and ignorance the Holy Spirit has to reveal in each of us.[2]

With the power of the Holy Spirit nourishing you, allow *Love Extravagantly* to be your personal trainer, showing you on what areas you need to work.

If you still find yourself repeatedly going back to old habits, you may need regular visits with a "personal trainer" to keep you accountable and offer guidance.

This is where a good change-oriented Christian counselor can be very effective. Just as some people can see heart-level changes in their Christian life by attending church and reading their Bible, others need the guidance and accountability of participating in a weekly Bible study. While some people can bring about change on their own, others need counseling. This does not make one a better or lesser person, but is merely an indication of our differences.

An unbiased third party can be very valuable: a friend, a marriage accountability group, a pastoral counselor, or a professional therapist. Chuck has found that many times a couple will leave a session happy with each other, but angry with him. Confronting others with their issues is a dirty job, but when a third party is involved, anger can be directed at the counselor and stay there rather than going home with the couple.

Marriage accountability groups can also supply valuable support to any marriage, from a couple ready to divorce to a couple that simply wants a deeper, intimate relationship.

> Being in a small group or desiring a healthy marriage, or committing to accountability in our lives is nothing new—but doing those three things together is. That's why the new paradigm of marriage accountability groups is built on a different set of values.[3]

Stephanie Janke has contributed to many of the scenarios in *Love Extravagantly*. As layleaders, she and her husband, Kurt, call their group "MAGNETS." MAG stands for marriage accountability group. The NET represents a "net" to catch them if they fall. Talking about their group, Stephanie says,

> The old paradigm embodied isolation, facades, fairness . . . judging, and/or silence, but the new paradigm suggests community, genuineness, integrity, growth, and speaking the truth in love. Just like going to the gym or losing weight, we seem to stick to the program better sometimes if we do it with friends.

If you find that you need the guidance and accountability that a third party can offer, Chuck has several suggestions for selecting a therapist that will help make the time with your "personal trainer" successful (appendix E).

Chuck worked with high-risk youth in a residential treatment facility. The boys he specifically worked with were all violent offenders who were one step away from jail. In the program they received their education, their meals, lodging, and therapy. For most of these teenagers, their only motivation to change was fear of consequences, resulting in first-order change at best. For the most part, the courts mandated their presence at the treatment center. The counseling appeared to do some good, but at the first opportunity they reverted back to their old ways—like the Sunday Christian, their change was on the surface. However, a few of the young men had become Christians somewhere along the line. By the power of the Holy Spirit, combined with the therapeutic efforts, real changes were made—changes that went from the head to the heart and played out in behavior.

For you, reading a book is a good first step—you understand the need for change, it is in your head. As a Christian, take advantage of the power that is available to nourish you and help you to make real changes, reorder your life, and turn from your old ways—a changed heart. Follow the insights and interactions outlined for you in the pages of *Love Extravagantly*. If you need the guidance and accountability a personal trainer or coach can provide, find a good Christian counselor.

Just as with your physical health, a combination of exercise, nourishment, and guidance from a professional yields the best results. Any personal-growth effort, including counseling, without the Holy Spirit gives only partial success. Yes, it is hard work. But like they say at the gym, "No pain, no gain."

Love Extravagantly

by Marita Littauer with Karen Lutgen

"Observe how Christ loved us.
His love was not cautious but extravagant.
He didn't love in order to get something from us
but in order to give everything of himself to us. Love like that."
(*Ephesians 5:2b*, THE MESSAGE)

There are times in our walk when we feel His presence;
He expresses His will, His love and His essence.
God speaks to our hearts in a dream or a vision;
In my case it came in the form of a mission.

As people will do with respect to career,
My professional life was defined and clear.
I established my mission, my purpose, my goals;
In my personal life, though, I sensed there were holes.

God gave me His insight, He showed me one day
That I was to demonstrate love in His way.
Extravagant love, not cautious or cheap,
A selfless love never seeking to reap.

A "mission impossible," wouldn't you say?
Self-serving and earning are touted—the way.
So each day I seek the Lord's help in my life;
I seek to excel in my place as a wife.

"Observe how Christ loved us"—He sacrificed all.
His life was a mission to break down the wall.
Not to get but to give so that I may win.
My mission it seems is to emulate Him.

Have you given some thought to your personal life?
Do you love extravagantly, husband or wife?
Consider God's vision for those marked as His—
Conformed to His image all hearts where He lives.

Appendix A

Your Personality Profile

On page 193, in each of the rows of four words across, place an X in the box in front of the one or two words that most often apply to you. Continue through all forty lines. If you are not sure which word most applies, ask your spouse or a friend, and think of what your answer would have been when you were a child. Use the following word definitions for the most accurate results.

Definitions of Strengths

(1) Adventurous One who will take on new and daring enterprises with a determination to master them.

Adaptable Easily fits in and is comfortable in any situation.

Animated Full of life; lively use of hand, arm, and face gestures.

Analytical Likes to examine the parts for their logical and proper relationships.

(2) Persistent Sees one project through to its completion before starting another.

Playful Full of fun and good humor.

Persuasive Convinces through logic and fact rather than charm or power.

Peaceful Seems undisturbed and tranquil and retreats from any form of strife.

(3) Submissive Easily accepts any other's point of view or desire with little need to assert his/her own opinion.

Self-sacrificing Willingly gives up his/her own personal being for the sake of, or to meet the needs of, others.

Sociable One who sees being with others as an opportunity to be cute and entertaining rather than as a challenge or business opportunity.

Strong-willed Determined to have one's own way.

(4) **Considerate** Having regard for the needs and feelings of others.

Controlled Has emotional feelings but rarely displays them.

Competitive Turns every situation, happening, or game into a contest and always plays to win!

Convincing Can win you over to anything through the sheer charm of his/her personality.

(5) **Refreshing** Renews and stimulates or makes others feel good.

Respectful Treats others with deference, honor, and esteem.

Reserved Self-restrained in expression of emotion or enthusiasm.

Resourceful Able to act quickly and effectively in virtually all situations.

(6) **Satisfied** A person who easily accepts any circumstance or situation.

Sensitive Intensely cares about others and what happens to them.

Self-reliant An independent person who can fully rely on her own capabilities, judgment, and resources.

Spirited Full of life and excitement.

(7) **Planner** Prefers to work out a detailed arrangement beforehand for the accomplishment of a project or goal and prefers involvement with the planning stages and the finished product rather than the carrying out of the task.

Patient Unmoved by delay, remains calm and tolerant.

Positive Knows it will turn out right if he/she's in charge.

Promoter Urges or compels others to go along, join, or invest through the charm of his/her own personality.

(8) **Sure** Confident, rarely hesitates or wavers.

Spontaneous Prefers all of life to be impulsive, unpremeditated activity, not restricted by plans.

Scheduled Makes and lives according to a daily plan; dislikes plans being interrupted.

Shy Quiet, doesn't easily instigate a conversation.

(9) **Orderly** Having a methodical, systematic arrangement of things.

Obliging Accommodating. One who is quick to do it another's way.

Outspoken Speaks frankly and without reserve.

Optimistic Sunny disposition. One who convinces self and others that everything will turn out all right.

Your Personality Profile

Strengths

1. ☐ Adventurous	☐ Adaptable	☐ Animated	☐ Analytical
2. ☐ Persistent	☐ Playful	☐ Persuasive	☐ Peaceful
3. ☐ Submissive	☐ Self-sacrificing	☐ Sociable	☐ Strong-willed
4. ☐ Considerate	☐ Controlled	☐ Competitive	☐ Convincing
5. ☐ Refreshing	☐ Respectful	☐ Reserved	☐ Resourceful
6. ☐ Satisfied	☐ Sensitive	☐ Self-reliant	☐ Spirited
7. ☐ Planner	☐ Patient	☐ Positive	☐ Promoter
8. ☐ Sure	☐ Spontaneous	☐ Scheduled	☐ Shy
9. ☐ Orderly	☐ Obliging	☐ Outspoken	☐ Optimistic
10. ☐ Friendly	☐ Faithful	☐ Funny	☐ Forceful
11. ☐ Daring	☐ Delightful	☐ Diplomatic	☐ Detailed
12. ☐ Cheerful	☐ Consistent	☐ Cultured	☐ Confident
13. ☐ Idealistic	☐ Independent	☐ Inoffensive	☐ Inspiring
14. ☐ Demonstrative	☐ Decisive	☐ Dry Humor	☐ Deep
15. ☐ Mediator	☐ Musical	☐ Mover	☐ Mixes Easily
16. ☐ Thoughtful	☐ Tenacious	☐ Talker	☐ Tolerant
17. ☐ Listener	☐ Loyal	☐ Leader	☐ Lively
18. ☐ Contented	☐ Chief	☐ Chartmaker	☐ Cute
19. ☐ Perfectionist	☐ Pleasant	☐ Productive	☐ Popular
20. ☐ Bouncy	☐ Bold	☐ Behaved	☐ Balanced

Weaknesses

21. ☐ Blank	☐ Bashful	☐ Brassy	☐ Bossy
22. ☐ Undisciplined	☐ Unsympathetic	☐ Unenthusiastic	☐ Unforgiving
23. ☐ Reticent	☐ Resentful	☐ Resistant	☐ Repetitious
24. ☐ Fussy	☐ Fearful	☐ Forgetful	☐ Frank
25. ☐ Impatient	☐ Insecure	☐ Indecisive	☐ Interrupts
26. ☐ Unpopular	☐ Uninvolved	☐ Unpredictable	☐ Unaffectionate
27. ☐ Headstrong	☐ Haphazard	☐ Hard to Please	☐ Hesitant
28. ☐ Plain	☐ Pessimistic	☐ Proud	☐ Permissive
29. ☐ Angers Easily	☐ Aimless	☐ Argumentative	☐ Alienated
30. ☐ Naïve	☐ Negative Attitude	☐ Nervy	☐ Nonchalant
31. ☐ Worrier	☐ Withdrawn	☐ Workaholic	☐ Wants Credit
32. ☐ Too Sensitive	☐ Tactless	☐ Timid	☐ Talkative
33. ☐ Doubtful	☐ Disorganized	☐ Domineering	☐ Depressed
34. ☐ Inconsistent	☐ Introvert	☐ Intolerant	☐ Indifferent
35. ☐ Messy	☐ Moody	☐ Mumbles	☐ Manipulative
36. ☐ Slow	☐ Stubborn	☐ Show-off	☐ Skeptical
37. ☐ Loner	☐ Lords Over Others	☐ Lazy	☐ Loud
38. ☐ Sluggish	☐ Suspicious	☐ Short-tempered	☐ Scatterbrained
39. ☐ Revengeful	☐ Restless	☐ Reluctant	☐ Rash
40. ☐ Compromising	☐ Critical	☐ Crafty	☐ Changeable

The Personality Profile was created by Fred Littauer and is taken from Florence Littauer, *After Every Wedding Comes a Marriage* (Eugene, Ore.: Harvest House Publishers, 1981). Used by permission. Not to be duplicated. Additional copies may be ordered by calling 800/433–6633 or visit www.thepersonalities.com.

(10) Friendly A responder rather than an initiator, seldom starts a conversation.

Faithful Consistently reliable, steadfast, loyal, and devoted, sometimes beyond reason.

Funny Sparkling sense of humor that can make virtually any story into a hilarious event.

Forceful A commanding personality. Someone others would hesitate to take a stand against.

(11) Daring Willing to take risks; fearless, bold.

Delightful A person who is upbeat and fun to be with.

Diplomatic Deals with people tactfully, sensitively, and patiently.

Detailed Does everything in proper order with a clear memory of all the things that happened.

(12) Cheerful Consistently in good spirits. Promotes happiness in others.

Consistent Stays on an even keel emotionally, responding as one might expect.

Cultured One whose interests involve both intellectual and artistic pursuits, such as theater, symphony, ballet.

Confident Self-assured and certain of own ability and success.

(13) Idealistic Visualizes things in their perfect form and has a need to measure up to that standard himself/herself.

Independent Self-sufficient, self-supporting, self-confident, and seems to have little need of help.

Inoffensive A person who never says or causes anything unpleasant or objectionable.

Inspiring Encourages others to work, join, or be involved and makes the whole thing fun.

(14) Demonstrative Openly expresses emotion, especially affection, and doesn't hesitate to touch others while speaking to them.

Decisive A person with quick, conclusive judgment-making ability.

Dry Humor Exhibits dry wit, usually one-liners that can be sarcastic in nature.

Deep Intense and often introspective with a distaste for surface conversation and pursuits.

(15) Mediator Consistently finds himself/herself in the role of reconciling differences in order to avoid conflict.

Musical Participates in or has a deep appreciation for music; is committed to music as an art form rather than the fun of performance.

Mover Driven by a need to be productive; is a leader whom others follow; finds it difficult to sit still.

Mixes Easily Loves a party and can't wait to meet everyone in the room; no one is a stranger.

(16) Thoughtful A considerate person who remembers special occasions and is quick to make a kind gesture.

Tenacious Holds on firmly, stubbornly, and won't let go until the goal is accomplished.

Talker Constantly talking; generally telling funny stories and entertaining everyone; feeling the need to fill the silence in order to make others comfortable.

Tolerant Easily accepts the thoughts and ways of others without the need to disagree with or change them.

(17) Listener Always seems willing to hear what you have to say.

Loyal Faithful to a person, ideal, or job, sometimes beyond reason.

Leader A natural-born director, who is driven to be in charge and often finds it difficult to believe that anyone else can do the job as well.

Lively Full of life; vigorous, energetic.

(18) Contented Easily satisfied with what she has, rarely envious.

Chief Commands leadership and expects people to follow.

Chartmaker Organizes life, tasks, and problem-solving by making lists, forms, or graphs.

Cute Precious, adorable, center of attention.

(19) Perfectionist Places high standards on himself/herself and often on others, desiring that everything be in proper order at all times.

Pleasant Easygoing, easy to be around, easy to talk with.

Productive Must constantly be working or achieving, often finds it very difficult to rest.

Popular Life of the party and therefore much desired as a party guest.

(20) Bouncy A bubbly, lively personality, full of energy.

Bold Fearless, daring, forward, unafraid of risk.

Behaved Consistently desires to conduct himself/herself within the realm of what he/she feels is proper.

Balanced Stable, middle-of-the-road personality, not subject to sharp highs or lows.

Definitions of Weaknesses

(21) Blank A person who shows little facial expression or emotion.

Bashful Shrinks from getting attention, resulting from self-consciousness.

Brassy Showy, flashy, comes on strong, too loud.

Bossy Commanding, domineering, sometimes overbearing in adult relationships.

(22) Undisciplined A person whose lack of order permeates almost every area of his/her life.

Unsympathetic Finds it difficult to relate to the problems or hurts of others.

Unenthusiastic Tends to not get excited, often feeling it won't work anyway.

Unforgiving One who has difficulty forgiving or forgetting a hurt or injustice, apt to hold on to a grudge.

(23) Reticent Struggles against or is unwilling to get involved, especially when such involvement is complex.

Resentful Often holds ill feelings as a result of real or imagined offenses.

Resistant Strives, works against, or hesitates to accept any other way but his/her own.

Repetitious Retells stories and incidents to entertain you without realizing he/she has already told the story several times before; is constantly needing something to say.

(24) Fussy Insistent over petty matters, calling for a great attention to trivial details.

Fearful Often experiences feelings of deep concern, apprehension, or anxiousness.

Forgetful Lack of memory, which is usually tied to a lack of discipline and not bothering to mentally record things that aren't fun.

Frank Straightforward, outspoken; doesn't mind telling you exactly what he/she thinks.

(25) Impatient A person who finds it difficult to endure irritation or wait for others.

Insecure One who is apprehensive or lacks confidence.

Indecisive The person who finds it difficult to make any decision at all (not the personality that labors long over each decision in order to make the perfect one).

Interrupts A person who is more of a talker than a listener, who starts speaking without even realizing someone else is already speaking.

(26) **Unpopular** A person whose intensity and demand for perfection can push others away.

Uninvolved Has no desire to listen or become interested in clubs, groups, activities, or other people's lives.

Unpredictable May be ecstatic one moment and down the next, or willing to help but then disappears, or promises to come but forgets to show up.

Unaffectionate Finds it difficult to verbally or physically demonstrate tenderness openly.

(27) **Headstrong** Insists on having his/her own way.

Haphazard Has no consistent way of doing things.

Hard to Please A person whose standards are set so high that it is difficult to ever satisfy them.

Hesitant Slow to get moving and hard to get involved.

(28) **Plain** A middle-of-the-road personality without highs or lows and showing little, if any, emotion.

Pessimistic While hoping for the best, this person generally sees the down side of a situation first.

Proud One with great self-esteem who sees himself/herself as always right and the best person for the job.

Permissive Allows others (including children) to do as they please so as not to be disliked.

(29) **Angers Easily** One who has a childlike flash-in-the-pan temper that expresses itself in tantrum style and is over and forgotten almost instantly.

Aimless Not a goal-setter, with little desire to be one.

Argumentative Incites arguments generally because he/she feels he/she is right no matter what the situation may be.

Alienated Easily feels estranged from others, often because of insecurity or fear that others don't really enjoy his/her company.

(30) **Naïve** Simple and childlike perspective, lacking sophistication or comprehension of what the deeper levels of life are really about.

Negative Attitude One whose attitude is seldom positive and is often able to see only the down or dark side of a situation.

Nervy Full of confidence, fortitude, and sheer guts, often in a negative sense.

Nonchalant Easygoing, unconcerned, indifferent.

(31) Worrier Consistently feels uncertain, troubled, or anxious.

Withdrawn A person who pulls back to himself/herself and needs a great deal of alone or isolation time.

Workaholic An aggressive goal-setter who must be constantly productive and feels very guilty when resting. Is not driven by a need for perfection or completion but by a need for accomplishment and reward.

Wants Credit Thrives on the credit or approval of others. As an entertainer, this person feeds on the applause, laughter, and/or acceptance of an audience.

(32) Too Sensitive Overly introspective, and easily offended when misunderstood.

Tactless Sometimes expresses himself/herself in a somewhat offensive and inconsiderate way.

Timid Shrinks from difficult situations.

Talkative An entertaining, compulsive talker who finds it difficult to listen.

(33) Doubtful Characterized by uncertainty and lack of confidence that something will ever work out.

Disorganized Lack of ability to ever get one's life in order.

Domineering Compulsively takes control of situations and/or people, usually telling others what to do.

Depressed A person who feels down much of the time.

(34) Inconsistent Erratic, contradictory; actions and emotions not based on logic.

Introvert A person whose thoughts and interests are directed inward; lives within himself/herself.

Intolerant Appears unable to withstand or accept another's attitudes, point of view, or way of doing things.

Indifferent A person to whom most things don't matter one way or the other.

(35) Messy Living in a state of disorder, unable to find things.

Moody Doesn't get very high emotionally, but easily slips into lows, often when feeling unappreciated.

Mumbles Will talk quietly under the breath when pushed; doesn't bother to speak clearly.

Manipulative Influences or manages shrewdly or deviously for his/her own advantage; will get his/her way somehow.

(36) Slow Doesn't often act or think quickly, too much of a bother.

Stubborn Determined to exert his/her own will, not easily persuaded, obstinate.

Show-off Needs to be the center of attention, wants to be watched.

Skeptical Disbelieving, questioning motives behind words.

(37) Loner Requires a lot of private time and tends to avoid other people.

Lords Over Others Doesn't hesitate to let you know that he/she is right or that he/she is in control.

Lazy Evaluates work or activity in terms of how much energy it will take.

Loud A person whose laugh or voice can be heard above others in the room.

(38) Sluggish Slow to get started; needs a push to be motivated.

Suspicious Tends to suspect or distrust others or ideas.

Short-tempered Has a demanding, impatience-based anger and a short fuse. Anger is expressed when others are not moving fast enough or have not completed what they have been asked to do.

Scatterbrained Lacks the power of concentration or attention; flighty.

(39) Revengeful Knowingly or otherwise holds a grudge and punishes the offender, often by subtly withholding friendship or affection.

Restless Likes constant new activity because it isn't fun to do the same things all the time.

Reluctant Struggles against getting involved or is unwilling to be involved.

Rash May act hastily without thinking things through, generally because of impatience.

(40) Compromising Will often relax his/her position, even when right, in order to avoid conflict.

Critical Constantly evaluating and making judgments, frequently thinking or expressing negative reactions.

Crafty Shrewd. One who can always find a way to get to his/her desired end.

Changeable Has a childlike, short attention span that needs a lot of change and variety to keep him/her from getting bored.

Personality Scoring Sheet

Transfer all your X's to the corresponding words on the Personality Scoring Sheets, and add up your totals. For example, if you checked Animated on the profile, check it on the scoring sheet. (Note: The words are in different orders on the profile and the scoring sheets.)

Personality Scoring Sheet—Strengths

	Popular Sanguine	Powerful Choleric	Perfect Melancholy	Peaceful Phlegmatic
1.	☐ Animated	☐ Adventurous	☐ Analytical	☐ Adaptable
2.	☐ Playful	☐ Persuasive	☐ Persistent	☐ Peaceful
3.	☐ Sociable	☐ Strong-willed	☐ Self-sacrificing	☐ Submissive
4.	☐ Convincing	☐ Competitive	☐ Considerate	☐ Controlled
5.	☐ Refreshing	☐ Resourceful	☐ Respectful	☐ Reserved
6.	☐ Spirited	☐ Self-reliant	☐ Sensitive	☐ Satisfied
7.	☐ Promoter	☐ Positive	☐ Planner	☐ Patient
8.	☐ Spontaneous	☐ Sure	☐ Scheduled	☐ Shy
9.	☐ Optimistic	☐ Outspoken	☐ Orderly	☐ Obliging
10.	☐ Funny	☐ Forceful	☐ Faithful	☐ Friendly
11.	☐ Delightful	☐ Daring	☐ Detailed	☐ Diplomatic
12.	☐ Cheerful	☐ Confident	☐ Cultured	☐ Consistent
13.	☐ Inspiring	☐ Independent	☐ Idealistic	☐ Inoffensive
14.	☐ Demonstrative	☐ Decisive	☐ Deep	☐ Dry Humor
15.	☐ Mixes Easily	☐ Mover	☐ Musical	☐ Mediator
16.	☐ Talker	☐ Tenacious	☐ Thoughtful	☐ Tolerant
17.	☐ Lively	☐ Leader	☐ Loyal	☐ Listener
18.	☐ Cute	☐ Chief	☐ Chartmaker	☐ Contented
19.	☐ Popular	☐ Productive	☐ Perfectionist	☐ Pleasant
20.	☐ Bouncy	☐ Bold	☐ Behaved	☐ Balanced

Strengths Totals

_____   _____   _____   _____

Personality Scoring Sheet—Weaknesses

Popular Sanguine	Powerful Choleric	Perfect Melancholy	Peaceful Phlegmatic
21. ☐ Brassy	☐ Bossy	☐ Bashful	☐ Blank
22. ☐ Undisciplined	☐ Unsympathetic	☐ Unforgiving	☐ Unenthusiastic
23. ☐ Repetitious	☐ Resistant	☐ Resentful	☐ Reticent
24. ☐ Forgetful	☐ Frank	☐ Fussy	☐ Fearful
25. ☐ Interrupts	☐ Impatient	☐ Insecure	☐ Indecisive
26. ☐ Unpredictable	☐ Unaffectionate	☐ Unpopular	☐ Uninvolved
27. ☐ Haphazard	☐ Headstrong	☐ Hard to Please	☐ Hesitant
28. ☐ Permissive	☐ Proud	☐ Pessimistic	☐ Plain
29. ☐ Angers Easily	☐ Argumentative	☐ Alienated	☐ Aimless
30. ☐ Naïve	☐ Nervy	☐ Negative Attitude	☐ Nonchalant
31. ☐ Wants Credit	☐ Workaholic	☐ Withdrawn	☐ Worrier
32. ☐ Talkative	☐ Tactless	☐ Too Sensitive	☐ Timid
33. ☐ Disorganized	☐ Domineering	☐ Depressed	☐ Doubtful
34. ☐ Inconsistent	☐ Intolerant	☐ Introvert	☐ Indifferent
35. ☐ Messy	☐ Manipulative	☐ Moody	☐ Mumbles
36. ☐ Show-off	☐ Stubborn	☐ Skeptical	☐ Slow
37. ☐ Loud	☐ Lords Over Others	☐ Loner	☐ Lazy
38. ☐ Scatterbrained	☐ Short-tempered	☐ Suspicious	☐ Sluggish
39. ☐ Restless	☐ Rash	☐ Revengeful	☐ Reluctant
40. ☐ Changeable	☐ Crafty	☐ Critical	☐ Compromising

Weaknesses Totals

_____ _____ _____ _____

COMBINED TOTALS

_____ _____ _____ _____

Once you've transferred your answers to the scoring sheet and added up your total number of answers in each of the four columns and your totals from both the strengths and weaknesses sections, you'll know your dominant personality type. You'll also know what combination you are. If, for example, your score is 35 in Powerful Choleric strengths and weaknesses, there's really little question. You're almost all Powerful Choleric. But if your score is, for example, 16 in Powerful Choleric, 14 in Perfect Melancholy, and 5 in each of the others, you're a Powerful Choleric with a strong Perfect Melancholy percentage. You'll also know, of course, your least-dominant type.

As you read and work with the material in *Love Extravagantly*, you'll learn how to put your strengths to work for you, how to compensate for the weaknesses in your dominant type, and how to understand the strengths and weaknesses of your spouse.

For additional information on The Personalities, read *Personality Puzzle, Getting Along With Almost Anybody,* and *Come As You Are,* all by Marita Littauer. They're available at bookstores, by calling 800-433-6633, or visiting www.thepersonalities.com.

An Overview of the Personalities

Popular Sanguines
"Let's do it the fun way."

Desire: have fun.

Emotional needs: attention, affection, approval, acceptance.

Key strengths: ability to talk about anything at any time at any place, bubbling personality, optimism, sense of humor, storytelling ability, enjoyment of people.

Key weaknesses: disorganized, can't remember details or names, exaggerates, not serious about anything, trusts others to do the work, too gullible and naïve.

Get depressed when: life is no fun and no one seems to love them.

Are afraid of: being unpopular or bored, having to live by the clock, having to keep a record of money spent.

Like people who: listen and laugh, praise and approve.

Dislike people who: criticize, don't respond to their humor, don't think they are cute.

Are valuable in work for: colorful creativity, optimism, light touch, cheering up others, entertaining.

Could improve if they: got organized, didn't talk so much, learned to tell time.

As leaders they: excite, persuade, and inspire others; exude charm and entertain; are forgetful and poor on follow-through.

Tend to marry: Perfect Melancholies who are sensitive and serious, but whom they quickly tire of having to cheer up and by whom they soon tire of being made to feel inadequate or stupid.

Reaction to stress: leave the scene, go shopping, find a fun group, create excuses, blame others.

Recognized by their: constant talking, loud volume, bright eyes.

Powerful Cholerics

"Let's do it my way."

Desire: have control.

Emotional needs: sense of obedience, appreciation for accomplishments, credit for ability.

Key strengths: ability to take charge of anything instantly and to make quick, correct judgments.

Key weaknesses: too bossy, domineering, autocratic, insensitive, impatient, unwilling to delegate or give credit to others.

Get depressed when: life is out of control and people won't do things their way.

Are afraid of: losing control of anything (e.g., losing a job, not being promoted, becoming seriously ill, having a rebellious child or unsupportive mate).

Like people who: are supportive and submissive, see things their way, cooperate quickly, let them take credit.

Dislike people who: are lazy and not interested in working constantly, buck their authority, become independent, aren't loyal.

Are valuable in work because they: can accomplish more than anyone else in a shorter time, are usually right.

Could improve if they: allowed others to make decisions, delegated authority, became more patient, didn't expect everyone to produce as they do.

As leaders they have: a natural feel for being in charge, a quick sense of what will work, a sincere belief in their ability to achieve, a potential to overwhelm less aggressive people.

Tend to marry: Peaceful Phlegmatics who will quietly obey and not buck their authority, but who never accomplish enough or get excited over their projects.

Reaction to stress: tighten control, work harder, exercise more, get rid of the offender.

Recognized by their: fast-moving approach, quick grab for control, self-confidence, restless, and overpowering attitude.

Perfect Melancholies

"Let's do it the right way."

Desire: have it right.

Emotional needs: sense of stability, space, silence, sensitivity, support.

Key strengths: ability to organize and set long-range goals, have high standards and ideals, analyze deeply.

Key weaknesses: easily depressed, too much time on preparation, too focused on details, remembers negatives, suspicious of others.

Get depressed when: life is out of order, standards aren't met, and no one seems to care.

Are afraid of: no one understanding how they really feel, making a mistake, having to compromise standards.

Like people who: are serious, intellectual, deep, and will carry on a sensible conversation.

Dislike people who: are lightweights, forgetful, late, disorganized, superficial, prevaricating, and unpredictable.

Are valuable in work for: sense of detail, love of analysis, follow-through, high standards of performance, compassion for the hurting.

Could improve if they: didn't take life quite so seriously, didn't insist others be perfectionists.

As leaders they: organize well, are sensitive to people's feelings, have deep creativity, want quality performance.

Tend to marry: Popular Sanguines for their outgoing personality and social skills, but whom they soon attempt to quiet and get on a schedule.

Reaction to stress: withdraw, get lost in a book, become depressed, give up, recount the problems.

Recognized by their: serious and sensitive nature, well-mannered approach, self-deprecating comments, meticulous and well-groomed looks.

Peaceful Phlegmatics

"Let's do it the easy way."

Desire: avoid conflict, keep the peace.

Emotional needs: sense of respect, feeling of worth, understanding, emotional support.

Key strengths: balance, even disposition, dry sense of humor, pleasing personality.

Key weaknesses: lack of decisiveness, enthusiasm, and energy; a hidden will of iron.

Get depressed when: life is full of conflict, they have to face a personal confrontation, no one wants to help, the buck stops with them.

Are afraid of: having to deal with a major personal problem, being left holding the bag, making major changes.

Like people who: will make decisions for them, will recognize their strengths, will not ignore them, will give them respect.

Dislike people who: are too pushy, too loud, and expect too much of them.

Are valuable in work because they: mediate between contentious people, objectively solve problems.

Could improve if they: set goals and became self-motivated, were willing to do more and move faster than expected, could face their own problems as well as they handle those of others.

As leaders they: keep calm, cool, and collected; don't make impulsive decisions; are well-liked and inoffensive; won't cause trouble; don't often come up with brilliant new ideas.

Tend to marry: Powerful Cholerics who are strong and decisive, but by whom they soon tire of being pushed around and looked down upon.

Reaction to stress: hide from it, watch TV, eat, tune out life.

Recognized by their: calm approach, relaxed posture (sitting or leaning when possible).

Appendix B

Marita's Famous Waffle Mix

Make up this mix and store it in the refrigerator in a jar or Ziploc bag. It will keep for up to a month, although it is certain to be used up before that. To use, simply combine ½ cup of mix with one egg and ½ cup of buttermilk, stir with a fork or spoon, pour into waffle iron, and cook according to manufacturer's instructions. The proportions listed here will perfectly fill a Nordic Ware Stove Top Belgian Waffler. You and your family will have a hot, healthy, wholesome breakfast with very little effort!

1⅓ cups rolled oats (such as Quaker)
½ cup whole wheat flour
2½ teaspoons baking powder
1 teaspoon baking soda
¾ teaspoon salt
¼ cup butter-flavored Crisco, or vegetable oil
2½ cups all-purpose or unbleached white flour

In a food processor, combine the first five dry ingredients until well mixed and the oats are finely ground. With the motor running add the shortening through the feed tube. Process using on/off pulses until the shortening is evenly incorporated, about one minute. You may need to stop to scrape down the bowl during this process. Add the white flour and combine using on/off pulses. Transfer to a jar or Ziploc bag for storage. Shake or stir once before storage to aerate the mix slightly. Store tightly sealed in refrigerator or freezer. Makes about 4½ cups of mix.

To use mix for pancakes, increase buttermilk to ¾ cup.

You can also make the mix with a blender or electric mixer. The oats will not be as finely ground.

Appendix C

Directory of Professional Contributors

Shellie Arnold
    Author, *Return to Eden Resources: Reclaiming God's Vision for Family Relationships*.
    1641 E. Sandpiper Trail
    Casselberry, FL 32707
    Shellie@returntoeden.net

Sylvia Burke, BSN
    Author, *Putting Humpty Dumpty Back Together Again*.
    25821 Bolero Ben
    Rio Verde, AZ 85263
    (480) 471–9617

Evelyn Davison
    Radio host, "LoveTalk," publisher, *Good News Journal*, author, *Praying for America's Leaders*
    Austin, Texas
    (512) 260-1800
    goodnews@aol.com

Roseanne P. Elling, M.Ed., LPC
    Family and Individual Therapist
    7103 Preston Rd., #288

Dallas, TX 75248
(972) 250-0498
(972) 250-0934 (FAX)
Roseanne2000@aol.com

Reese Gateley, CPA
Tax and financial statement preparer and consultant for individuals and business.
2901 Juan Tabo NE, Suite 117
Albuquerque, NM 87112–1885
(505) 296–8891
(505) 296–9509 FAX
gatecpa@flash.net

Andrea Golzmane, MA, LMFT
The New England Center for Marriage and Family Therapy
335 Walnut Street Extension, Suite 200
Agawam, MA 01001–1524
(413) 789–8955
(413) 789–0557 FAX

Michelle A. Holman, MA, LPC
Christian Life Coach
Her Life, Inc.
2007 Collins #405
Richardson, TX 75080
(214) 575–8686
(972) 234–3089 FAX
www.michelleholman.net
connect@michelleholman.net

G. Victoria Jackson, MSW, LCSW
Over thirty years of family counseling experience.
Teacher, cultural diversity and social work, Loma Linda University.
Contributing author, *Understanding Intimate Violence.*
Co-founder, Touch of Class—a Christian charm course for teens in San Bernardino, CA.
vjackson@univ.llu.edu

Stephanie and Kurt Janke
Walk in the Spirit
2476 S. Queen St.
York, PA 17402
(717) 741-9518

Ruth L. Kopp, M.D.
Author, *Encounter With Terminal Illness* (with Stephen Sorenson), reissued as *When Someone You Love Is Dying*, Zondervan 1980; *Where Has Grandpa Gone?* Zondervan, 1983.
Family practice physician, emphasis on counseling.
328 South 4th Street
Pekin, IL 61554
(888) 275–9766
(309) 347–1109 FAX
drruthmd.com
drruth@drruthmd.com

Gaylen B. Larson, Ph.D.
Founder, California's largest professional counseling service, author, speaker, consultant.
28202 Cabot Road, Suite 253
Laguna Niguel, CA 92677
(949) 474–4888
www.AskDoctorGaylen.com

Derryn Lowrey, RN, MSN
tlowrey@nm.net

Maxine Marsolini
Author, *Blended Families, Creating Harmony as You Build a New Home Life*, Moody Press 2000.
Pastor's wife
(541) 831–1080
www.webmaxine.com

Chuck Noon, MA, LPCC
P.O. Box 66810
Albuquerque, NM 87193
www.chucknoon.com

Susan M. Rogers, MA, LPC
Director of CHPM Counseling Center
2301 Midwestern Parkway, Suite 212
Wichita Falls, TX 76308
(940) 696–0181
smrogers@iolwf.com

Georgia Shaffer, MA
Author, *A Gift of Mourning Glories: Restoring Your Life After Loss*, Servant
Publications 2000.
Pennsylvania-licensed Psychologist
Member of American Association of Christian Counselors
Executive Director of Mourning Glory Ministries
P.O. Box 3113
York, PA 17402–0113
(717) 266–4773
(717) 266–7481 FAX
www.GeorgiaShaffer.com
Georgia@MourningGlory.org

Rose Sweet
Author, *How to Be First in a Second Marriage*, College Press 1998, *Healing the
Heartbreak of Divorce*, Hendrickson Publishers, 2001.
Pastoral counselor, member American Association of Christian Counselors
73–241 Hwy 111, #3D
Palm Desert, CA 92260
(760) 346–9401
(760) 340–9430 FAX
Nuqween@aol.com
www.rosesweet.org

Mary Hunt Webb, MA
   Adult Learning and Training Specialist
   P. O. Box 14462
   Albuquerque, NM 87191–4462
   mamswebb@highfiber.com

Melanie R. Wilson, Ph.D.
   Licensed Psychologist, New Life Clinics of St. Louis
   Director of Marital Preparation, Christ Memorial Lutheran Church
   9712 Tesson Ferry Road
   St. Louis, MO 63127
   (314) 631–0304
   www.drmelaniewilson.com
   melphd@aol.com

Appendix D

The Couple's Communication Exercise

Consider how you learned to communicate. Think of your family of origin where the parents talked *at* the children. In school, the teacher talked *at* the students. Perhaps you participated in classroom debate where persuasive speech was an asset. Throughout college and on into the work force, the skill of persuasive speech was rewarded. However, the skills that are functional in other aspects of our lives can be counter-productive within the marriage environment.

Therefore, in preparation for growth within the marriage relationship, the weakest part of our communication skills (listening) must be developed. Where before we were either speaking or thinking about what we were going to say next, instead we will learn to focus on the other person. This basic skill for improved communication is called "active listening." In this process, we are not thinking about our response to what was said. We are not thinking about whether what our spouse is saying is right or wrong or even if we agree or disagree. We are only striving to hear and understand the words that are being spoken.

From a Personality standpoint, some people inherently talk too much and others too little. The following exercise is designed to make communication a two-way street between opposite Personalities. As in tennis, the ball should go back and forth, spending equal amounts of time on each side of the court with each party alternating turns. We are not advocating that this be the daily communication model; rather, this is a specific exercise designed to strengthen a designated skill.

The Communication Exercise

This active listening exercise begins with person "A" making an "I" statement: "I feel," "I think," "I am," etc. The primary objective is to avoid the word "you."

Husband and wife alternate playing "A" and "B." Chuck recommends that this "I" statement be constructed in a brief and concise three-point outline. Both parties need to turn toward each other and maintain eye contact throughout delivery of the statement. For example, using the scenario from chapter 2, Joan would face John, look him in the eye, and say, "I feel alone, neglected, and I really need more time together."

The goal for person B (this play John, next play Joan will be "B") is to strive to function as a tape recorder, reflecting back only what was said in an impartial manner. Person B should preface his response with "What I heard you say was . . ." Therefore, the complete response would be, "What I heard you say was, you are feeling alone, neglected, and you need more time together." Then, person B should always close his reflection with "How did I do?" This sets the stage for a subjective response from person A. It says, "I care more about what you feel than being right (or wrong) myself." Marriage is not a court of law; couples must get away from establishing truth or fact, and move on to pleasing each other.

Person A, Joan, should make a judgment call at this point. Either she is happy with the reflection or it fell short of her expectation. If she was happy with it, she says, "Very good," and the first play of the exercise is done. However, in reality a more common response from person B would be, "You think I am neglecting you and I work too much"—which is not at all what she said. As in this case, if the reflection is inaccurate or involves a judgment, she should say, "That is not quite what I had hoped to communicate. May I tell you again?" This last, "May I tell you again?" is said with enthusiasm. This process continues until person B gets it right. Chuck has found that couples sometimes will go through a dozen cycles before a simple statement such as we have illustrated here is accurately reflected. This in itself is a victory.

Next, the husband becomes person A. He presents his feelings on a fresh tack, without responding to her statement or defending himself. For example, he might say, "I feel trapped. At work they always want more. At home I feel guilty." She now responds, as person B, by reflecting exactly what he said, "What I heard you say is, you feel trapped. At work they always want more. At home you feel guilty."

This may seem contrived and elementary. However, many times Chuck has seen an exchange like the one above when a spouse says with excitement, "Yes! That's exactly what I've been trying to tell you for six years!" In other cases, person "A" will say in reflection, "Did I say that? I don't think that!" Most people have no idea how they sound to other people. Most people will not even recognize their own voices recorded on a tape recorder!

Once each partner has successfully stated their feelings and reflected them back to the other party several times, the exercise is complete. No resolution takes place at this stage. The goal is simply to exercise the listening skill, which will pay off in many other settings. In fact, whenever a party recognizes that their communication has become dysfunctional, this is a good fallback position to get back on track. It is virtually impossible to fight in this format.

The goal is for the marital relationship to become a mirror of the self. A mirror reflects a face in an impartial manner. Only within the intimacy of a healthy marriage (or therapy)—can we begin to throw out our innermost thoughts and feelings, and examine them out in the open.

In most communication settings outside of marriage, the listener does not have our best interest in mind. What others say to us is focused on how they can persuade or control us. The marriage should be a safe haven from the world where we must surround ourselves with shields. However, within the marriage we must learn to lower these shields.

Appendix E

Selecting a Therapist

In receiving counseling you are in essence buying an intangible product. While the product (your marriage and/or your mental health) is of great value, its intangible quality makes it difficult to think of paying for it. You are dealing with your life; do not take the cheapest route.

First, screen your therapist. Ask the therapist about his or her education. Did she receive her training from a reputable institution with time-tested successes or was she involved in a home-study type program? Does the program have the accreditation or approval of organizations such as the American Association for Marriage and Family Therapy (AAMFT)? Was there a practicum in the program where the student counseled people while under the "live supervision" of a professor? Next, ask about his internship. Where was this done? What type of licensed therapist provided supervision? Were there mentors? At what point did he select a theoretical orientation? How is the therapist licensed? What is the therapist doing in continuing education? Ask the therapist/candidate: "What is your theoretical model of how change occurs?" There are many good answers here; any number of tools properly implemented will do the job. However, most therapists will not even understand the question, or will not have a clear answer. Look for a therapist who is excited about the change-oriented process.

Next, inquire about the therapist's motivation. Chuck remembers his education:

My professor of law and ethics said the cleanest motivation for a therapist to perform therapy was in exchange for payment. The therapist does his job well and in return the customer pays a fee. This was controversial in our class. Most of my classmates felt that the motivation for therapy should be more altruistic. I agree with my professor. Beware of the therapist who is driven to "help people."

Many of those with the greatest personal pathology feel the greatest need to meddle in other people's lives. Their own unresolved issues unavoidably color their patient's therapy.

Next, look at your own motivation. Do you have a real desire for change? Most people seeking professional help say they want to change when what they really want is relief from the consequences of their actions, an alleviation of symptoms. Some people do not want to change at all; they merely want an affirmation of their actions, or they seek counseling to humor someone else. If the therapist is unable to "fix" the problem, the client can then report that they tried: "I went to counseling, but it didn't work." The person who desires a real heart change invites the Holy Spirit into the process: "He convinces of sin; He illuminates and instructs."[1]

To make the best of your investment in counseling, be sure that you have a well-trained Christian therapist who has a change-oriented approach. Ask for referrals to find a therapist who has healthy motivation. Last, be sure that you go into counseling with a right attitude—allowing the Holy Spirit to convince you of sin, illuminate it, and instruct. While psychotherapy can fail, it doesn't have to.

Notes

Preface
1. Glenn T. Stanton, *Why Marriage Matters* (Colorado Springs: Pinion Press, 1997), 165.

Chapter 1
1. Justice Sandra Day O'Connor, quoted in *San Diego Union Tribune*, June 11, 2000.
2. If you are unfamiliar with my teaching on The Personalities—Popular Sanguine, Powerful Choleric, Perfect Melancholy, and Peaceful Phlegmatic, please read appendix A before going on.
3. Karen S. Peterson, "Teachers Schooled in Family Ties," *USA Today*, August 21, 2000, 5D.
4. "U.S. Has Far Fewer Traditional Families," *Arizona Republic*, 1999.

Chapter 3
1. *Life Application Bible* (Wheaton, Ill.: Tyndale House, 1997). This excerpt taken from a software version.
2. Peter Mayle, *Encore Provence: New Adventures in the South of France* (New York: Alfred A. Knopf, 1999), 79–80.

Chapter 4
1. Michelle McKinney Hammond, *The Power of Femininity* (Eugene, Ore.: Harvest House Publishers, 1999), 233.

Chapter 6
1. For more information on this concept, read Marita Littauer and Chuck Noon, "Which Personality Is the Best to Marry?" *Getting Along With Almost Anybody* (Grand Rapids, Mich.: Revell, 1998.

2. *Life Application Bible* (Wheaton, Ill.: Tyndale House, 1997).
3. "Points to Ponder," *Reader's Digest*, October 1999, 125. Quoted from *Life* magazine.

Chapter 9
1. Gary Thomas, *Sacred Marriage* (Grand Rapids, Mich.: Zondervan Publishing House, 2000), 115.

Chapter 11
1. Dorothy Patterson, general editor, *Women's Study Bible* (Nashville: Thomas Nelson Publishers, 1995), 1583.
2. Gary Thomas, *Sacred Marriage* (Grand Rapids, Mich.: Zondervan Publishing House, 2000), 161.

Chapter 12
1. Patterson, ed., *Women's Study Bible*, 71.
2. Karen S. Peterson, "Teachers Schooled in Family Ties," *USA Today*, August 21, 2000, 5D.
3. Russell Baker, *Growing Up* (New York: Penguin USA, 1995).
4. Thomas, *Sacred Marriage*, 250, 262.

Chapter 13
1. Glen T. Stanton, *Why Marriage Matters* (Colorado Springs: Pinon Press, 1997), 158.
2. Thomas, *Sacred Marriage*, 261.

Chapter 14
1. Thomas, *Sacred Marriage*, 251, 35.
2. Dan Allender and Tremper Longman, *Intimate Allies* (Wheaton, Ill.: Tyndale House, 1995).

Chapter 16
1. Article to be published in *Light and Life*, date undetermined.
2. Walter Trobisch, *I Married You* (San Francisco: Harper & Row, 1971), 20–21.

Chapter 17
1. Willard Harley, *His Needs, Her Needs* (Old Tappan, N.J.: Fleming H. Revell, 1986), 41.
2. Stormie Omartian, *The Power of a Praying Wife* (Eugene, Ore.: Harvest House Publishers, 1997), 65.
3. Omartian, *The Power of a Praying Wife*, 61–62.
4. Omartian, *The Power of a Praying Wife*, 45.

Chapter 18
1. Joanna Weaver, *Having a Mary Heart in a Martha World* (Oxnard, Calif.: WaterBrook Press, 2000), 159.

2. Oswald Chambers, *My Utmost for His Highest*, An Updated Edition in Today's Language (Grand Rapids, Mich.: Discovery House, 1992), reading for January 13.

3. Jeff and Lora Helton, *Authentic Marriages: How to Connect With Other Couples Through a Marriage Accountability Group*, 36.

Appendix E

1. Charles Spurgeon, *Morning and Evening* (Bible Explorer Software), reading for October 12, evening.

Acknowledgments

The most important person to thank when writing a book on marriage is one's spouse. Thank you, Chuck, for working with me on this project. It has been wonderful to work side-by-side with you. Thank you too for allowing me to make your life public. I hope reading about our struggles and solutions will help other couples apply the love extravagantly principle in their own marriages.

Thank you to my friends and family who allowed me to tell their stories.

Thank you to the thousands of people on my e-mail list who have read the scenarios I posted weekly while I was working on this book and who have contributed their own stories. Your input lets the readers know they are not alone. You deserve special thanks for being willing to read each draft of the various chapters and then offer your comments and editing advice. You have made this a better book.

Thank you to the "professionals" who have read each scenario and offered their valuable insight to help couples who are struggling.

Thanks to Steve Laube and Julie Smith of Bethany House for their direction, guidance, and editing—even when I did not want to be directed, guided, and especially, edited! We make a good team!

—*Marita Littauer*

Thanks to Selvini Palazzoli and the Milan Associates for developing "Milan Systemic" family therapy, and to Jay Haley for "Brief Strategic" family therapy. These theoretical bases heavily influenced me during my education and in practice as a therapist. After this book began to take shape, I realized that Marita too had incorporated these approaches into formulating and solving problems. Most of all, thank you to my wife, Marita. Ecclesiastes 9:9 (TLB) counsels us: "Live happily with the